M&A Basics

For Cannabis & Hemp Companies

A Company Owner's Guide to Key Deal Elements
& Common Practices of Mergers & Acquisitions

John D. Wagner

Dr. Carl Craig

1stWest M&A Press
Colorado

CONTENTS

- Preface: **A Cannabis & Hemp Market Prospective**
    - Page 6

- Chapter 1: **Considering Selling Your Business? Here's How to Prepare**
    - Page 10

- Chapter 2: **Your Business is Worth What Someone Will Pay for It**
    - Page 27

- Chapter 3: **How Best to Go to Market**
    - Page 31

- Chapter 4: **With Markets Strong, Should You Delay Selling?**
    - Page 36

- Chapter 5: **Can You "Time the Market" When Selling?**
    - Page 40

- Chapter 6: **Acquirers Want Leadership Continuity**
    - Page 45

- Chapter 7: **What Happens to Real Estate If Your Acquired?**
    - Page 51

- Chapter 8: **Trailing Twelve Months Earnings**
    - Page 55

- Chapter 9: **That's Not a Downward Trend. Let's Normalize Revenue**
    - Page 60

- Chapter 10: **What's Your Customer Concentration?**
  - Page 65
- Chapter 11: **Maintaining (and Increasing) GPMs**
  - Page 70

- Chapter 12: **Maximize Business Value with Credits to EBITDA**
  - Page 74

- Chapter 13: **What Are Earnouts? How Do They Work?**
  - Page 79

- Chapter 14: **Earnings Quality and the Buyer's Right to Know**
  - Page 84

- Chapter 15: **How Much Cash Must You Leave Behind?**
  - Page 89

- Chapter 16: **The (Irksome) Due Diligence Process**
  - Page 95

- Chapter 17: **Are You Too Ready to Sell?**
  - Page 101

- Chapter 18: **Asset Sale or Stock Sale?**
  - Page 106

- Chapter 19: **Leave Profanity and Politics at the Door**
  - Page 111

- Chapter 20: **"Pricing In" a Recession**
  - Page 115

- Chapter 21: **Can Your Company be Re-Priced After the LOI?**
  - Page 120

- Chapter 22: **Why Do Deals Fall Apart?**
  - Page 122

- Chapter 23: **How to Communicate News of a Deal**
  - Page 130

- Chapter 24: **How Investment Bankers Get Paid**
  - Page 135

- **About the Authors**   Page 140
- **About 1stWest M&A**   Page 142
- **Glossary of Terms**   Page 144

M&A Basics

Copyright 2019
All rights reserved
Printed in the USA

Wagner, John, D.
Craig, Carl

M&A Basics For Cannabis & Hemp Companies
A Company Owner's Guide to Key Deal Elements
& Common Practices of Mergers & Acquisitions

ISBN: 9781795527972

All rights reserved. No part of this publication may be reproduced, stored in
a retrieval system or transmitted in any form without the prior written permission of the authors.

First Edition

Printed in the USA

02, 03, 04, 05, 06, 07, 08, 09

M&A Basics

Preface:

A Cannabis & Hemp Market Prospective

Mergers and acquisitions activity in the cannabis and hemp sector is the most active it has ever been, and it will only get hotter with each passing month. The drivers of such intense activity – and the reasons for today's strong company valuations – are broadcast via headlines in every major news outlet in North America: It's the broad (*and growing*) legalization of cannabis and hemp products.

For hemp in the U.S., the 2018 Farm Bill legalized hemp throughout all 50 states for the first time. For cannabis, the legalization has been rolling across the land on a state-by-state basis. As this book is headed to the printer, in early 2019, eleven U.S. states have legalized both medical and recreational marijuana. Twenty two additional states have legalized medical marijuana. In total, 32 states and the District of Columbia have some form of legalized marijuana. Other states will soon follow.

And then there's Canada, where the legalization has been on a national scale. The estimated size of the Canadian marijuana market ranges between $4 and $6 billion U.S. dollars for 2019. It will only grow over time.

What's equally remarkable about the cannabis and hemp sectors is the *company valuations* that are being achieved in mergers and acquisitions activity. But take note of something interesting that's happening: Even as cannabis and hemp products are coming out of the shadows of illegality, the metrics by which these companies are values are remarkably traditional. Indeed, they are the same metrics that have been used for decades to establish the values of other companies, entirely unrelated to cannabis and hemp. Such performance metrics as *gross profit margins*, *EBITDA*, *OPEX,* and *COGs* are all used in the cannabis and hemp sector, just as they are in other industries. That said, there *is* something unusual and non-traditional about the cannabis and hemp sectors, and that's high valuations achieved in the sales of these companies. Those valuations (the *total enterprise values* paid to acquire cannabis and hemp companies) are being paid not just on historical company performance; instead, there is often a *premium* paid for the *expected growth* in cannabis and hemp markets. That growth is not limited just to retail operations that are marketing cannabis and hemp products, but in other areas as well, such as laboratory and compliance testing services, regulatory compliance equipment, and infrastructure for farming operations needed to grow and process cannabis and hemp at industrial scales.

When you recognize that the 2018 market size for cannabis and hemp in *Nevada alone* was $615 million, and that Oregon was $650 million, and that Colorado was $1.7 billion, you don't need an MBA from Harvard to recognize that these large-volume industries need support services of a magnitude we have historically seen in "big pharma" or industrial farming. That's true whether services are focused on product creation, product packaging, product transportation, or product testing. So, it's really not a surprise to see cannabis and hemp mergers and acquisition activity spike up the way it is trending now.

How this book works: This book presents two dozen chapters to help you navigate the cannabis and hemp mergers and acquisitions process. We have a bias for the "sell side" of M&A (advising companies that are offering themselves for acquisition), and in this book we cover the basics of preparing a company for that acquisition process. But the business principles we cover are just as applicable if you are an acquirer. (We have advised acquirers as well). So, there is something within these pages for every aspect of the industry.

In these chapters, we outline how to position a company for the highest possible value, and we lay out what you can expect during the entire arc of the acquisitions and due-diligence processes. See what you can learn from our experience. If you need to know more, we welcome contact from you, using the information in the back of this book; or just visit our company's website.

John D. Wagner

Carl Craig, Ph.D.

www.1stWestMA.com

> *"Success usually comes to those who are too busy to be looking for it."*
>
> — Henry David Thoreau

Chapter 1

Considering Selling Your Business? Here's How to Prepare

Most business owners who contact us to inquire about selling their businesses ask the same two opening questions.

1. "What metrics are used to determine the value of my business when a buyer is looking to make an acquisition?"

2. "What are the top three or four steps I can take to maximize that value?"

Even in the cannabis and hemp sector – whether your company is a laboratory, a grower, a farm, a retail business, or a provider of cannabis and hemp derivative products – buyers all value the same basic performance metrics of a company. (These metrics are easy to identify, which we shall do forthwith.) Once a business owner determines that it's time to prepare for a sale, it is a relatively straightforward task to optimize the sale value of the company by focusing on improving these metrics. That said, businesses can't be changed overnight. If you are selling your business, and there are aspects of operation that need attention, you will likely need some lead time (perhaps six months or more, depending on the quality of your advisor) to get your house in order. Let's take a closer look.

Where to Focus?

During your preparation period, as you move toward offering you company for sale, focus on improving the productivity and performance of your business, both top line (gross revenues) and bottom line (net profit). Keep in mind that potential buyers will scrutinize your financial statements for the last *three years*. They will also examine "trailing twelve months" financial statements, expecting continuous financial performance over these periods of time. You will achieve the highest valuation when you show consistent year-over-year improvement. A business that books, say, $15 million in business for each of the last three years, with good net margins, may be very attractive to you, the business owner, but the value of that company will be heightened if the business experiences consistent, predictable *year-over-year* growth, in addition to solid financial performance, typically measured by a stronger *percent EBITDA* (the percent of gross revenue that ends up as net earnings), discipline in maintaining gross profit margin, and discipline in controlling expenses, like "SG&A" expenses – *selling, general and administration.*

It may come as a surprise that traditional basics used to value old-line businesses are also used today in cannabis and hemp transactions, even though the cannabis and hemp industry is relatively new and, in the case of cannabis, coming out of the shadows of illegality. In other words, there are no special rules for cannabis and hemp companies, aside from, perhaps, a premium that might be paid for these companies because of the speed with which these markets are expanding. Nonetheless, most buyers will look for what they have always looked for: 1) a solid balance sheet with excellent A/R (showing little or no account dating and low delinquencies; 2) good cash flow; 3) high quality earnings, and a *percent EBITDA* that meets or exceeds industry norms. These are among the primary drivers in the valuation process, and it's these metrics that should be your top priority when preparing your company for a potential sale.

"Well-Presented...Half Sold"

In addition to getting the financial aspects of the business in order, it is also essential that your financial performance be well-documented. Well-presented financial statements that use standardized GAAP methods of accounting go a long way to giving your buyer confidence that you are running a high-performance company. Just having your financials in order can actually heighten values almost as much as solid earnings, because the buyer will think: "Heck, if they've got their financial statements in such good shape, I'll bet the rest of the business is equally well cared for."

Further, as you prepare for sale, an internal SWOT analysis (*Strengths, Weakness, Opportunities & Threats*) can be a useful tool in determining what aspects of the business need improvement. (Within the SWOT analysis, S (Strengths) and W (Weaknesses) refer to internal factors in your company that you can control. O (Opportunities) and T (Threats) are typically outside the control of your business but directly impact your business.). In fact, a potential buyer of your business will more than likely perform their own SWOT analysis, so you can only imagine how impressive it will be if you get ahead of the curve and perform your own to show that you are working to improve the business, even as you prepare to sell it.

Timing

Timing the sale of your business is based on many factors, but two are critical. You want to sell your business when it is doing well *and* the industry sector is healthy. Just as an unprofitable business has little value in a good economy, a company with historically strong earnings will not achieve its highest value if it is sold when the economy is on the decline or in the tank. If your business is cyclical industry, or you work in a sector of the industry that is subject to changing regulations and an unpredictable tax landscape (especially true of cannabis and hemp), you have to ask yourself: Am I prepared to wait out the next downturn, or to chance some unforeseen regulatory hurdles? Or should I sell now, knowing that the sale process will take around six months to a year to complete?

A solid economic environment that is at its peak, or even near its peak — on its way *up*, not on the way down! — is an ideal time to engage a mergers and acquisitions advisory team to help prepare your business and put it on the market to see what valuations you could achieve.

There are external factors, such as the overall economy, global events, and industry business cycles, which are not in your control, and it's probably a mark of prudence (and not stupidity) to take your exit in a safe business environment, even if you potentially leave a "little bit of money on the table."

For example: If your business is worth between 5X and 8X multiple of adjusted EBITDA today—that's a typical multiple range for our cannabis and hemp sectors for an all-cash deal, although valuations can go much higher with multi-year earnouts—that multiple can *easily* drop in a down cycle, where you would see a 5X multiple of adjusted EBITDA *or lower*. At 5X, you would need to increase your EBITDA by 40% just to get back to a dollar valuation equal to the 7X multiple of EBITDA in an up-market cycle. Selling today at, say, 7X, even when you suspect you could achieve a higher value, would likely be a great move in retrospect if the economy were to constrict or regulation and tax laws were to change.

Valuations

Is your business special? Sure it is! Just like a homeowner who puts his or her house on the market and expects that it will achieve a premium value because it is "special," almost every business owner thinks their business should achieve a multiple of value in excess of the averages being paid today. That's not necessarily a bad position to hold. It shows that you, the owner, takes great pride in what you've achieved over many years of hard work building up the business. That said, in preparation for the sale of your business, it is important to understand the valuation process and have a realistic expectation of the valuation range.

What's realistic? You can readily secure a valuation range from the investment banking firm representing you in the sale of your company. But that investment banking firm really should have an understanding of the idiosyncrasies of the cannabis and hemp-related business sectors. So, it's important that your M&A advisor demonstrate that expertise, along with the normal and traditional practices required to get any deal done, in or out of cannabis and hemp. For instance, when researching valuations, if your investment banker pulls down values for *pharmaceutical testing labs*, when he should have looked specially at *cannabis testing labs*, that error could result in you leaving a substantial sum of money on the table. That's because these two types of companies may be selling at different multiples of earnings. Even small errors in valuation estimates can have dramatic effects on the company value obtained in a sale, as we will cover later in this book.

Where do M&A advisors M&A advisor get the values being paid today? There are databases available to investment bankers and brokers that show the actual valuations of the sale of businesses similar to yours that have recently sold. Since M&A activity in the cannabis and hemp business is relatively new, note that your M&A

advisor may have to triangulate deals done in closely related industries as the valuation data builds up over time.

Knowing the *average valuation range* being paid for businesses like yours is a critical initial step, but it represents an *average* and not necessarily what you will get in terms of valuation for your business. Whether you receive offers below, at average, or a premium above the average valuation range will all depend on factors beyond just the financial performance of your business. Here's a list of some of these factors:

- **Market Strength at the Time of Sale**: Is your sub-sector within the cannabis and hemp markets strong? Are the long- and short-term prospects for your sub-sector strong? That will have a direct impact on the valuations paid for your business, and make no mistake, the acquirer's analysts will spare little expense to determining those prospects very precisely. Other factors that affect valuations are many, including interest rates, material costs, the cost of labor, the cost of healthcare and pension programs, and even the cost of fuel or utilities.

- **Strength of the Management Team**: A buyer of your business will very likely want to keep the team in place that made the company as strong as it is today. If you have a strong "bench" of management talent, and they're willing to stay with the company after the sale, that will heighten the value of your business. If you have a leadership team that is going to vacate their offices as soon as the transaction is complete, that will devalue your business, at least equal to the replacement costs of that missing talent. Good management, solid succession planning, and leadership continuity invariably lead to a higher price paid for your company.

- **Market Position and Competitive Landscape**: If your business is in a crowded market and you are fiercely competing for new clients, and/or fiercely competing to keep legacy clients, this will cause a downward pressure on your valuation. A buyer will look at where you are in the competitive landscape and determine your relative strengths against other businesses in your region or those that compete with you. A solid market position, or a dominant presence in a competitive landscape will help you achieve the highest value possible.

- **Product Mix and Services**: If your product or services mix is overly concentrated in one area, that lack of diversity may not attract a shrewd buyer. Buyers like to see a balanced mix of products and services to show that the company is diversified, thereby lowering risks. If you have a good mix, it demonstrates that you have managed your company well, and this should be reflected in a high valuation.

- **Customer Concentration**: If you have one customer who accounts for more than 10% of your business, or one customer whose loss would affect earnings in a meaningful and negative way, a buyer will devalue your business accordingly. A diverse customer base is essential to a good valuation.

- **Asset Quality**: The quality of the assets being sold will impact the multiple on your earnings. A company that has driven up its earnings by foregoing maintenance (on building, land, or equipment), shorting inventory, or undermining the strength of its management team with non-market-rate salaries, is not going to be as attractive as a company that takes care of its equipment, its inventory, and its employees.

- **Quality of Earnings:** Are your earnings sustainable and is a meaningful amount of your business predictably repeating? Or was a great recent year a "sugar high" of earnings, which is unlikely to repeat? Non-repeating business is more expensive to obtain than repeat business, and that's something that we be examined in detail by a buyer.

The M&A Process

The *controlled auction:* Selling your business is a one-time event and one of the most important business decisions that you will make. The execution of the sale of your business must be done with the utmost professionalism if you are to optimize its value. That process typically starts with a M&A advisory firm (sometimes called an *investment banker* or *broker*) preparing an *Informational Memorandum* that builds a narrative around your business and explains the various financial declarations that are contained in the *Informational Memorandum*. (The *Informational Memorandum* is also called an "IM." So people call it an OM for *offering memorandum*; some people call it a *deal book*).

In addition to presenting and describing your financials, leadership profiles, and competitive landscape, among other aspect of your business, the *Informational Memorandum* should tell a powerful story about your company, its history, and its culture. Done well, the *Informational Memorandum* should not only be well written, but look good graphically as well.

- As the preparation process is completed and outreach is made to the broadest possible community of buyers, the M&A advisory firm should extract a premium valuation (with acceptable terms and conditions) through a *controlled auction* to a group of serious and pre-qualified buyers. Under this controlled auction approach, in a process entirely managed by your M&A advisory firm, buyers privately bid against one another for your business, while you decide what is the best offer, based on your sales objective.

- Your M&A advisory firm should identify all potential qualified acquirers ("targets") who may have an interest in acquiring your business. It is not unusual for the list of potential targets to number in the hundreds or even thousands. There are databases that tell which strategic and financials buyers have been active in your sector, and your M&A advisor should have access to these resources.

- In addition to the *Informational Memorandum*, your M&A advisory firm should prepare a one-page "teaser" that is initially sent to each of the targets. The teaser summarizes your business, and lists recent financial performance without actually naming your business. Many targets try to guess who you are, but the teaser is designed to reveal basic financial performance and the industry sector, hoping to get targets interested in seeing the IM.

- Confidentiality Agreements (CAs) are sent along with the "teaser" by the M&A advisory firm. No IMs should be sent until the CAs are signed.

- o Note that, as a seller, you have veto power over who gets to see the teaser. So, *carefully review* the outreach list ahead of time. It's a little embarrassing if a target responds to a teaser with a signed Confidentiality Agreements, only to have the investment banker go back and say, "Oops, sorry, we shouldn't have sent you the teaser in the first place.)
- Once everything is in place, outreach is made, usually via email, and your business goes to market.

Getting Started with the M&A Process

Surrounding yourself with a strong advisory team to manage the sales process is critical to achieving your sales objective, and that team allows you to run your business during the sales process. Here are three key components to put in place as you go to market:

- An M&A advisory firm (your investment banker) that really understands your business and the cannabis and hemp market. M&A advisory firm should have the staff to prepare and execute the methodology and steps described in this book. M&A advisory is not done well by a one-person operation. Look for a firm that has executed a substantial number of high-value deals, in and out of cannabis and hemp.

- A transaction attorney who specializes in M&A transactions and can handle the Letters of Intent and Sales Agreements (a.k.a. *Asset Purchase Agreement*, or *Definitive Purchase Agreement*) once you decide on the winning acquirer. An attorney with specialty knowledge of the cannabis and hemp businesses is essential, given today's highly regulatory environment, and how regulations can vary state by state. Do not use the lawyer who drafted your will, or reviewed your real estate lease. The legal practice of M&A transactions is a specialty practice.
- An accountant who can generate the reports and financial documentation required of a sale.

There is no more exciting time in the life of the business owner than when he or she can sell a business for meaningful profit after many years of building the business value. The cost of hiring an M&A advisor (explained in this book) is a small price to pay to prepare your business for sale, to make it as attractive as possible to a potential buyer, to maximize the value obtained, and to allow you to run your business successfully during the process.

"If you can't explain it simply, you don't understand it well enough."

– Albert Einstein

Chapter 2

Your Business is Worth What Someone Will Pay for It

There is a person we know who has a nice house she needs to sell. She asked us to take a look at it and tell her, just ballpark, what she should list it for.

We walked through the house —*nice place!*—but in a rural setting, far from town. We said it would be a stretch, but that she should list it for $400,000.

"$400,000!?" she shrieked. *"No way!* That's a special house. I have to get $650,000 for the cash I need, and that's what I'm listing it for."

That was three years ago, and it's still on the market, dropping $10,000 each time she changes realtors.

In our mergers and acquisitions practice, that same dynamic occurs when a buyer calls our firm. Early on, we ask, *Have you thought about what you want for the business?* It's not unusual to hear, *Well, I need to get $10 million.*

Then we ask, *How did you arrive at that figure?*

And the seller says, *Well, I need to pull $100,000 a year for my retirement, pay off my bank notes, and settle up with the IRS. I figure I'm going to live another 15 to 20 years. So I need $10 million to make the numbers work.*

Just like the overpriced house, that's a business that may still be on the market three years from now, waiting for a buyer who agrees with the $10 million value.

The homeowner and the business owner had a value in their mind before the fair market values were calculated realistically.

Like it or not, a house or a business is worth what someone will pay for it, not what the owner needs for retirement.

Your business is your baby. You've invested time building it up. You've added facilities and capabilities, while nurturing a great staff. Maybe you've even eaten bad debt and skipped a vacation or two so you had enough cash to hand out Christmas bonuses. You're right to expect a reward for your hard work. But that recognition will come through the *performance* of your business, the *quality* of your earnings, and the *sustainability* of the business on a go-forward basis.

What Really Motivates a Buyer?

Typically, a prospective buyer will be motivated initially by the strategic fit of your business, e.g. your product lines, customer mix, and geographical reach. If those requirements are met, the buyer will engage in a financial analysis, which looks at the sales, gross profit margins, OPEX, and EBITDA margin trends over the last three years. They will also want your projections for the coming year. Additionally, the leadership team you have assembled and the workplace culture you have established play an important role in boosting the quality of your earnings, and those contributions should not be minimized.

As for value, in most industries, including cannabis and hemp, valuations are based on a multiple of adjusted EBITDA. When selling your business, we counsel taking a good look at the financials, and—given today's multiples, which are easy to determine—arrive at a realistic value that fully accounts for your earnings and for the intangibles you may bring to the valuation equation. The job of your investment banker is to fight fiercely to maximize that value. Additionally, every good investment banker firm should, as a matter of course, discover value-enhancing features and credits to EBITDA that which might be missed by the seller. That said, your expectations should be ultimately tied to your financial statements, and not what you "need to get" out of the transaction. The financial statements are where your hard work and sacrifice are most-accurately reflected, and that is what will be ultimately rewarded with the highest possible value for your company.

"You miss 100% of the shots you don't take."

– Wayne Gretzky

Chapter 3

How Best to Go to Market

We use to work for a large manufacturer, and the executive in charge had a saying that's always stuck with us. Whether we were preparing the presentations, he'd say, *Well-presented, half sold.*

That's true for boardroom presentations, but it's also true when you are selling your company. The presentation of the company, typically in the form of an *Informational Memorandum,* along with accompanying financial statements and tax returns, are viewed as an indicator of the *overall* state of the company and its operations.

Just as you would no more respect a salesman who was sloppy in his communications, late to appointments, or who wasn't dressed properly for a meeting, so too you would hold suspicious a company going to market with haphazard financial statements, or one that had paid no real attention to creating an attractive information-rich *Informational Memorandum*.

A prospective client recently asked us: *What's the one thing we should do to prepare for a sale of our company?*

Is it boosting earnings? Sure, that helps. But it's not the #1 item.

Is it to ensure leadership continuity? Essential to have, yes, but not at the top of the list.

Is it paying off debts? Debt-free companies are certainly attractive.

However, when going to market, there's something even more important, and that's to get your *financial statements* in order so that your balance sheets and profit-and-loss (P&L) statements are *clean and well-presented* in standard formats.

What's more, you will need these statements for the last three years along with statements detailing your *trailing twelve months* to be sure to capture good performance even if you are in the middle of a fiscal year. In addition, you will need to prepare projections for the rest of the current year and for the next fiscal year.

Presenting these statements in GAAP accounting formats (*general accepted accounting principles*) will make sure that they can be easily read, even by someone who is not familiar with the idiosyncrasies of your company or of the cannabis and hemp industries. *That's well-presented.*

With information that's well-presented, your investment banker (and any potential buyers) can compare one year to any other year, and easily calculate such values as year-over-year progress, compounded annual growth rates for revenues, EBITDA, percent EBITDA, and year-to-date performance. This can be done in multiple categories, including gross profit margins, operating expenses, operating income, and bottom line earnings.

Clean well-presented statements also make it easier to argue for *and defend* adjustments to EBITDA for non-recurring expenses that won't be assumed by the new owner, but which boost the value of your company, sometimes dramatically. (More on that later in this book.)

Additional items you will need to have in "pin clean" presentation mode are, if applicable, any inventory statements—knowing that they will be physically redone just before the deal closes—a list of other assets, and your recent tax returns.

A "One-Page" Approach

Our firm recently worked with a company we took to market, and a prospective buyer wanted to see a list of assets, to understand, as he put it, "everything that would be ours if we wrote you a check today."

Impressively, we had it at-the-ready, in a one-page format. And that's what elicited the following comment from the prospect: "Gosh, it's nice to see everything on one page."

That's well-presented.

Of course, you can't present every aspect of the company in one-page formats. But a distillation of data in a condensed presentation goes a long way toward assuring this prospective buyer that:

1. The seller knows the assets are and how much they are worth.

2. The prospective buyer could trust the seller to produce, on-demand, all the summary data and documents that he or she needs to review when appraising the value of his potential purchase.

Plainly stated, it builds trust.

How do you create these clean documents, in formats even complete strangers can readily understand? Work with your accounting firm and directly with a CPA. If you are doing the books yourself in a system like QuickBooks, you may find that the statements drawn from in-house use of QuickBooks are not going to be adequate. So, invest the money and the time for an accounting firm to create the genuine articles. Because… *Well-presented, half sold.*

> *"Luck is the residue of design."*
>
> *– Branch Rickey*

Chapter 4

With Markets Strong, Should You Delay Selling?

Let's say the cannabis and hemp sectors are roaring at the time you are reading this book. Everyone's doing great, and party confetti seems from the ceiling every time you look at your monthly sales reports. Projections indicate that this will continue to be a great year or two as the cannabis and hemp sectors open up across the nation.

Lots of business owners we talk to ask us, "With the markets going so well, should I sell now? Or should I ride the economy up for a couple more years?"

As much as everyone understands that the worse time to sell a business is during a bad economy, people generally don't hold the reciprocal perception that a strong economy is a great time to sell a business. That's because everyone thinks the party will go on forever.

The fact is, most industries (*like most economies!*) are cyclical. Make no mistake, a good market will cycle down, and experience shows that when the music stops, there's not going to be enough chairs for everyone to grab a seat in time.

That's when we tend to get calls from business owners who—emotionally or financially unwilling to endure a downturn—will say, "I probably should have called last year, because now I have to wait out another down cycle, or sell for less today."

While your business may not be exactly at its peak today, it may be wise to start thinking about taking an exit ramp, especially if you feel exhausted, or are getting older and want to work more on your fishing or golf skills than spend Saturdays with your bookkeeper. No matter when you sell, there will always be a niggling fear that you left a little money on the table… but what's that old business cliché? *You've made a smart move if you sold just before the peak.*

Do the Math

Let's take a look at the effects of a drop of 2X in valuation (from a 7X to a 5X) due to a faltering economy, or any other reason. And for ease of math, let's say that you were earning $1,000,000 in EBITDA. That drop in multiple from 7X to 5X means that someone who was going to pay $7,000,000 for your business ($1,000,000 X 7) will now be willing to pay $5,000,000 ($1,000,000 X 5).

If you sell at 5X, you would need to increase your EBITDA by 40% just to get back to a *dollar valuation* equal to the 7X multiple you might have obtained in a good market. If your EBITDA is $1,000,000 today, you'd have to generate an EBITDA of $1.4 million *in a down market* at 5X to get the same value for your company you'd get today at 7X with a $1,000,000 EBITDA. We're sure it goes without saying that increasing EBITDA by 40% in a down market would be an extraordinary accomplishment.

Given how long it takes to complete a deal—the journey from the *Informational Memorandum* draft to the *definitive purchase agreement / deal closing* can take up to a year—should you sell today, near the peak? Or risk waiting out another cycle to get a higher value? A *middle path* might be to start preparing now, by obtaining a valuation of your business from an outside M&A advisory firm/investment banker, and perhaps even test the market to see whether offers might be forthcoming. You can always say "no," or, if presently surprised by a strong offer, say "yes."

(Note: A thorough, independent valuation from an M&A advisory firm/investment banker usually runs around $5,000 and should include a written report.)

> *"If you don't know where you are going, you might wind up someplace else."*
>
> – Yogi Berra

Chapter 5

Can You "Time the Market" When Selling?

"Timing the market" is something that every investment counselor advises against for your personal finances, and it's no different for selling your cannabis and hemp businesses. In fact, any prudent mergers and acquisitions advisor would recommend against trying to time the market. The reason is simple: The only thing you be can sure about in any economy is what is going on *right now*. Global events are beyond our control; a cataclysmic disaster (another 9-11) or natural disaster (earthquake or flood) can set economies reeling. And that's to say nothing of the unpredictability of accidents at your business location, or family emergencies, or the volatility of cannabis and hemp regulation with changing governmental leadership.

So, timing the market for the sale of your business may be a matter of simply *acting now*.

Invariably, the reason business owners wait to sell their business is because they want to grow it to get a higher value. Fair enough, but let's look at a scenario where the market takes a bit of a downturn and see how that would wipe out any incremental growth that you were able to achieve.

In good economies, the multiple of earnings paid for the acquisition of typical cannabis or hemp businesses is between 5X and 7X adjusted EBITDA for a deal that pays all cash-at-close. (Multiples can be much higher if the seller shares some risk with the acquirer, e.g. in multi-year earnouts.) That 5X to 7X range is not something arbitrary. It's obtained from databases that base their information on actual deals completed over the previous 12 months, and year-to-year it's fairly consistent.

No matter what the going multiple is in the year of your sale, a *strategic buyer* who is acquiring a competitor or complimentary business pays the high end of that multiple range (sometimes paying a premium *over* 7X), while financial buyers, such as venture funds, private equity groups, or so-called "family offices" (entities that manage a private family's money) typically pay the low end of the range.

Assuming a 5X – 7X range, what happens to that 7X in a downturn if you don't time your sale correctly? It drops, obviously. If the economy tightens even a little bit, that multiple might move to 6X, 5X, or much lower. What are the implications of this downturn? (As just mentioned, if your business is worth a 7X EBITDA today, but drops to 5X in a sour market, you would need to increase your EBITDA by a whopping 40% just to get back to a dollar valuation equal to the 7X multiple being used in today's market.)

In Hindsight, I Wish I'd...

Obviously, you want to sell your business when it is doing well *and* the industry sector is healthy. Just as an unprofitable business has little value in a good economy, a company with historically strong earnings will not achieve its highest value if it is sold when the economy is on the decline or in the tank. Selling today at a 7X, even when you suspect you could achieve a higher value, would likely be a great move in retrospect if the economy were to constrict in the year after a sale.

Finally, no matter the state of the market, be realistic. We can't tell you how often a seller comes to our firm with an unrealistic value expectation in mind, and then they turn down a truly reasonable offer when the buyer's offer doesn't come up to that figure . Regardless of market conditions, or what period of the business cycle you offer your company for sale, the first step is to set a realistic price for your company. As an M&A advisory, all the investment bankers in our firm are always clear *early on* about what we think we can obtain, given current market conditions. If the seller believes we are setting our sights too low, yet we know we are being realistic, we often recommend that they consider engaging another advisor.

Knowing the price range being paid, *and* having everyone agree on what's reasonable, is a critical early step in the selling process.

With that consensus, the seller and the advisory team can work together with confidence and set realistic goals for the sale.

"I failed my way to success."

– Thomas Edison

Chapter 6

Acquirers Want Leadership Continuity and Succession Planning

Think of your business as if it were a large tactical ship. Now, imagine a potential acquirer of that ship admiring it from the shore.

"Wow," the fellow says, "look how well that ship runs! The officers in charge manage it perfectly!" Everyone looks up in awe as it sails by. *"I've got to buy it!"* he says.

Next thing you know, the acquirer makes a successful offer. He can't wait to get aboard and meet the great leadership team and crew…only to be disappointed when he walks onto the bridge to see that all the officers have left.

His first words would be: "Who's going to run this operation? Where's the captain? And where's that great executive officer? I thought I was buying the ship and the entire team!"

This reaction upon finding the ship's empty bridge is no different than you would see from someone who acquired your company only to find out that the leadership had all jumped ship when the transaction closed.

We all know that the leadership of a company—as well as the "crew" they assemble and the culture they establish—are what make a company successful. It's that leadership team the acquirer needs to move the company forward. The acquirer wants to take advantage of their institutional knowledge and their relationships to employees, the brand, the vendors, and the banks. In short, acquirers want *leadership continuity*, and if there is no leadership continuity, the acquirers want to see a sophisticated, highly professional process of *succession planning* to guarantee leadership performance through a leadership transition.

Without exception, in the absence of leadership continuity or succession planning, acquirers will either walk away, or severely devalue a leaderless or poorly led company. For starters, that devaluation will likely take the form of docking you, the seller, for the replacement costs of the executives he or she has got to hire anew upon taking charge (salary, benefits, bonuses, and all compensation), and even the costs of making that talent acquisition through a head hunter.

What the Experts Say

Tony Misura, president of the Misura Group, a leading executive recruitment firm, understands the importance of leadership succession.

If you want the executive succession to be factored into the valuation of the sale, acquirers will want to see the trailing three year's financials, during which the future leaders *of the company had significant authority*, Tony recently told us.

Naturally, if an acquirer likes those financials, they'll want to keep the leadership that put up those numbers. And if some of that leadership is not going to stay on under new ownership (e.g. when owners cash out), then those leaders have to be replaced by new people that the acquirer believes have the talent to steer the ship in the future.

Tony adds, *Keep in mind that putting a solid team in place can be a three- to four-year process. If you've made the wrong hire in the run-up to the sale of the business, you need enough time to determine if a particular hire was ill-advised. Harvard Business Review reported that Fortune 500 leaders run about 50% success rate on hiring decisions.*

The lesson here is clear: Don't wait until the last minute to install a new team that will remain in place post-acquisition. The leadership should be an integral part of the success of the operation that's being acquired, and they should have been in place for a meaningful period of time—surely enough time to prove that they are the right team to make the operation a continued success. What's more, the leadership team that will remain in place must know about the potential pending sale of the company. You can only imagine the damage control you'd have to do if you suddenly broke the news to the management team that you've sold your company, only to have half of them storm off, resentful that they weren't kept in the loop. Even after you let them know of the sale, you may have to incentivize the team with "stay bonuses" to keep them interested through the transition to new ownership.

Family Involved?

Ensuring leadership continuity and succession planning can have added complications if the business is family-owned and family-run. When multiple family members own different percentages of the company, and some want to leave and some want to stay on, it is probably advisable that an impartial (non-family-member) consultant be involved in constructing the go-forward leadership team *and* that advisor should be vested with some power.

Although Granddad and Dad might have done a great job building up the company over the decades, Junior might not be the executive material that an acquirer wants in place. If a family insists that Junior be the new CEO, and the acquirer isn't exactly thrilled with that prospect, the acquirer may devalue the company accordingly or entirely lose interest and walk away.

This is where that dispassionate outsider can step in, preserve the value that is at risk of being lost, and get the right leaders installed. Even with the most structured system in place, it's hard to avoid awkward family conversations. But it's better to have those conversations now, rather than in the heat of the sale of your company.

> *"Almost all quality improvement comes via simplification..."*
>
> *– Tom Peters*

Chapter 7

What Happens to Real Estate If Your Acquired?

Many businesses we speak with about mergers and acquisitions own the buildings and land where their businesses operate. Sometimes a separate LLC or incorporated business owns the real estate; sometimes it's owned by the business; and sometimes it's owned personally by you, the business owner. In any event, many businesses pay rent to themselves or to their own real estate holding company.

No matter how the real estate is held, most businesses that want to be acquired usually desire to sell the real estate with the business, as part of one clean package.

Only one problem.

Most buyers want to acquire your business for the cash flow. They don't want to invest, say, $1 million or more in real estate that doesn't contribute meaningfully to their earnings. Most will resist "becoming their own landlord."

Who can blame them? Parking that much capital in real estate makes a big portion of their investment, essentially, *dead money*. So, when preparing to sell your business, it usually makes sense to create an LLC or corporation that owns the real estate *separately* from your business operations. In this arrangement, the operation, no matter who owns it, pays rent to the holding corporation. (Many companies already have this arrangement in place.)

Steps to Prepare

If you are preparing to sell your business, before going on the market, work with your investment banker to get the land and buildings appraised. In most cases, even though the acquirer would prefer not to own the land or the buildings, it is prudent to split out the appraised value of your holdings categorically, so you can agree on a reasonable rent.

Get appraisals for fair market *sale value* and fair market *rent value*. With these figures in mind, the corporation that owns the real estate can set lease terms, no matter who pays it. Note that these rent and sale values are often subject to challenge at bargaining time in the acquisition process, so be fair and get substantive multiple opinions to arrive at a current "FMV" (*fair market value*).

How Rent Affects Value

Next, you have to consider how the rent affects the value of your company. Keep in mind that when you sell your business, the rent you have been paying has been charged against the business, so it was an operating expense and it is already "baked into" the EBITDA calculation. (The EBITDA is the figure to which a multiple is applied when determining the value of your business.)

It is important that you are currently charging a FMV rent to the business that can be validated through a FMV rent analysis, through a third party. Under a long-term lease arrangement with the new ownership, they will insist on a FMV rent. If you are charging the business now with higher than FMV rent, it will be adjusted to FMV rent and will be a negative adjustment to EBITDA. If you are charging the business below FMV rent, the new ownership may try to hold that rent and you will be renting to the new ownership *under* FMV rent. To take this issue off the table during negotiations, it is simply best to make sure you are charging FMV rent to the business.

In summary, as much as you would like to just sell the entire operation to a new owner—including the buildings and land—that rarely happens. Most acquirers will want a lease-back, like a *triple new lease* (taxes, most maintenance, and rent), rather than park their capital in real estate where it is not actively generating a return. Finally, note that most investment bankers will count the dollar value of the lease in the TEV (*total enterprise value*) of the deal, and that lease value will be included in the calculation of the investment bankers' success fee.

"If you really look closely,

most overnight successes

took a long time."

– Steve Jobs

Chapter 8

Trailing Twelve Months Earnings

Let's say it's October 1st, and you are in the process of selling your company. Let's also say that your financial statements are prepared on the basis of a calendar year (January 1 to December 31). In other words, you are still three months shy of completing your fiscal year.

Let's also assume that you are having a *killer year* in sales. My goodness, you haven't put up sales numbers in years! Salespeople have a snap in their step; there's a gleam in the eye of the sales VP, and everyone's feeling confident. What's more, since you've taken strong steps to control your costs in recent years, the strong sales figures are contributing to a healthy bottom line. Your company earnings have not ever looked this good.

Since you are selling your company, the main question on your mind is simple: *Even if we have not completed the current fiscal year, how can we use these strong current earnings in the calculation of our company's valuation? How can we avoid tying our value solely to the last completed fiscal year?*

Your concern is very real, and it can mean the difference between taking home a great sum of money or leaving a pile of it on the table.

To underscore the importance of this issue, let's do some quick math. Let's say that companies like yours are being acquired for multiples of around 7X adjusted EBITDA.

Knowing that multiple, get your calculator and run some numbers. For every $100,000 you add to your EBITDA, you are rewarded with an additional $700,000 in company value at the time you are acquired.

If your EBITDA in the last fiscal year was $1,000,000, and you're acquired for 7X, then the *total enterprise value* (TEV) of your company is $7,000,000.

If you had added $100,000 to the EBITDA, your company value would have been $1,100,000 x 7, or $7,700,000, a very nice lift indeed. In other words, you are essentially getting $7 in increased TEV for every $1 you add to EBITDA.

If it's October, and your current year is not yet complete, you surely have sales projections for the rest of the year. Projections are well and good, but an acquirer will want to see actual EBITDA, on a historical basis; they have only so much faith in projections. After all, investors are naturally cautious. (Who knows what could happen in the remaining months of the year? A weather calamity? Faltering health of a key company owner? A terrorist attack?)

The path to obtaining the valuation boost you deserve for strong ongoing earning is a *trailing twelve months* earnings calculation, also known as "TTM."

By presenting TTM to a potential acquirer, you are essentially showing the results of your last 12 months of performance, but not your last calendar year. Instead, you are showing them EBITDA from, *per se*, a *rolling Fiscal Year* that ends on the last day of every previous month. Very simply put: TTM rewards you for your very latest earnings performance.

As you move deeper into your company's "real" complete year, you should still calculate your TTM after every month, whether you are selling your company or not. Be sure to load in *all* your ongoing costs; don't wait until year-end, because you'll be deceived by phantom earnings.

With the TTM calculation, you also have your finger directly on the pulse of your business. You can detect—practically in *real time*—if the company's earnings are turning sour and need help, or when earnings are going through the roof, confirming that you're on the right track. Waiting to the end of the calendar year to calculate EBITDA doesn't give you much chance for a mid-course fix, unless you've mastered the ability to go back in time, and everyone knows only Michael J. Fox and Doc Brown can do that.

Finally, TTM is a widely accepted metric in the mergers and acquisitions sector, since it reflects your actual performance over the last twelve months. By using TTM, and insisting that you get a multiple of earnings on your current sales, and not those from a year ago, TTM can help you ask for the highest possible value for your business at the time of sale.

"If you are not embarrassed by the first version of your product, you've launched too late."

— Reid Hoffman, co-founder of LinkedIn

Chapter 9

That's Not a Downward Trend! Let's Normalize Revenues.

One of the worst red flags for an acquirer is when they see your revenues drop in the year you sell your company compared to the previous year. Even worse is the following scenario: You show a good solid symmetrical increase in revenues over a *number of years*, only to have revenues go soft just before a sale.

For example, assume that you want to sell your company this year. Looking back over three years financials, let's say that your company booked $20 million three years ago, then $22 million two years ago, and then – a banner year! – $27 million last year.

That's a nice growth path. You added $2 million and then $5 million to your revenue. What's not to like?

But let's also say that in the year of sale your revenues *declined* to $26 million. Even though your company has experienced solid gains in revenue growth – moving from $20 to $26 million over three years – it appears as though your revenues are falling from $27 million to $26 million year-over-year at the time of sale.

Since we obviously don't have data about next year's sales, a $1 million drop is sales year-over-year will be perceived as the *beginning of a downward trend* by an acquirer that is looking for any reason to lower the purchase price of your company.

How do you argue for maximum valuation, when your company seems to be losing marketshare? The answer: Normalizing your revenues.

In a situation like this, your investment banker should dig deeply into the reasons why your $27 million year was so strong…and an anomaly. Maybe a new cannabis or hemp regulation got enacted, and there was pent up demand. That one-time occurrence was a fantastic boost in your revenues. Let's say it was $3 million in unexpected revenue. You know it was a "sugar high" that may not repeat, but why should you be punished in the valuation of your business just because of this one-time event?

The best approach to take here is to have your investment banker write an explanation of this in the *Informational Memorandum* (the document that describes all your operations and financials). The investment banker should make a bar chart or infographic that shows that what's *really* happening to your company is the following: You are growing at the rate of $2 million a year. You booked $20 million three years ago, $22 million two years ago, $24 million (*normalized*) last year, and $26 million this year.

Inevitably the acquirer will say, "Wait, you didn't book $24 million last year. Says right here in the financials that you booked $27 million!"

You and your investment banker should respond: "We actually booked $24 million in a normalized revenue projection and – as you can see with this evidence we have presented – a huge one-time burst of action gave us an anomalous boost of $3 million in revenue."

Since you are not going to have your valuation pegged to last year's revenue (or only partially so), it actually behooves you to show symmetrical $2 million increases rather than to reveal a phantom "downward trend" in revenues represented by the "drop" from $27 million to $26 million.

Why wouldn't you want to take credit for that sugar high of on unusual incremental $3 million boost in revenue? Isn't it better to just own that as evidence that, well, it might happen again?

As nice as it is to show such strong recent revenues, acquirers want revenues and growth that are *sustainable*. The sustainability allows them to plan and predict. If they know that a company will increase sales by $2 million a year, that's marginally more attractive from a planning point of than revenues that are asymmetrical, up one year, down the next.

All of that said, can you get credit for a $3 million flush of orders from another new development in your service area? You certainly can. In the Informational Memorandum, a good investment banker will have surveyed forthcoming new projects / planned projects, and baked in the possibility of you obtaining that work in the future. Although those future revenues are not nearly as valuable as actual booked revenue, they show promise for your markets, and that should help infuse a sense of optimism in the mind of the acquirer, which will probably affect the valuation in positive way.

> *"People who succeed have momentum. The more they succeed, the more they want to succeed, and the more they find a way to succeed. Similarly, when someone is failing, the tendency is to get on a downward spiral that can even become a self-fulfilling prophecy."*
>
> *– Tony Robbins*

Chapter 10

What's Your Customer Concentration?

Imagine if you had only one customer. Make no mistake, it would have to be a *big* customer to keep your business busy. But with only one customer, you'd have only one income stream. And you'd be extremely watchful of that customer's purchasing behavior, because your entire business would be dependent on them. Everything that happened to that customer, good or bad, would happen to you.

So, why not spread the risk?

Of course, that's exactly what you do in your business today, by selling to hundreds, if not thousands, of customers each month. By doing so, you lower the chances that a loss of any one customer would have a catastrophic effect on your business.

It's important not to have too much revenue financial concentration among your biggest clients, especially if the collapse of just a few of them would mean the failure for your entire company.

The Reveal

If you ever seek an acquirer, the *Informational Memorandum* that your investment banker produces to take your company to market will have a section that reveals your *Customer Concentration*. It's a crucial and telling section of the *Informational Memorandum*, because every potential acquirer will want to see how much of your business would drop away if you lost a few of your biggest buyers.

Is heavy concentration at the top really a bad thing? Not necessarily, if those top customers are stable and pay on time. You'd probably be surprised to see how many companies have as much as 40% or more of their business concentrated in a dozen customers. In fact, if you're lucky, some large customers can actually be less costly to serve, and it's a benefit to do a great deal of business with them. They often have technology (e.g. mobile portals for managing purchase orders) to smooth out delivery and payment schedules. Plus, your invoicing might be simpler when you are sending a superbill to a national-grade accounting department, with a strong cash position and a seven-figure credit line. High-quality receivables from large buyers can be an asset, not a liability... until there is *too much* concentration in too few accounts. That might make an acquirer a little nervous, generating a request for more detail about the nature of the customers you are dealing with at that level. (As a rule of thumb: No one customer should represent more than 10% of your business.)

Discounting at the Top

In addition to looking at revenue concentration among your top customers, a potential acquirer will also want to see the gross profit margin (GPM) for *each* of those customers. Their interest in the GPMs is more than just idle curiosity. The acquirer wants to know if you are heavily discounting to your high-volume buyers. If you are, that's a source for some concern, because you may be delivering large volumes of product at very low margins, a scenario that would ding your company valuation.

However, if your GPMs are around the same as the GPMs you are achieving from your other customers, that shows you run a tight ship, and that you've stuck to your guns when negotiating price, even with your high-volume purchasers. That's one sure sign of a well-run business.

If you have not calculated your customer concentration, it would be an instructive exercise to engage in today. Calculate your GPMs for your top customers, and while you are at it, compare those figures to the GPMs of your lowest-revenue customers to see how they stack up by comparison. If you are preparing to sell your company, make adjustments now, as much as you can. Then, when you are finally ready to show your books to a potential acquirer, you'll have the data to readily put their concerns about customer concentration to rest.

"If you define yourself by how you differ from the competition, you're probably in trouble."

– Omar Hamoui, AdMob

Chapter 11

Maintaining (and Increasing) GPMs

It's hard to underscore enough the importance of maintaining consistency with your *gross profit margins* (GPMs) over a period of years. In every deal we are involved in, the acquirer looks at the consistency of GPMs as an indicator of the health of the business. And well they should. GPM consistency shows, among other things, that you have disciplined cost controls and are adding value to the products and services you provide to your customers.

To look at this from the acquirer's perspective, consider this example. If three years ago you had a GPM of 30%, and then it dropped to 27% the following year, and ticked back up to 28% in the current year, that would be perceived not exactly as erratic, but as a variance you should have taken more steps to control.

For ease of math, let's say you have a multi-location business that is booking $100 million in total "topline" revenue. If your GPM is 30%, then $30,000,000 is your gross profit. Let's also say that you lost control of some of your *cost of goods* expenses. For example, you put a pay increase in place to keep key employees, or you had to lower the price of certain products to be competitive. Any time you have an expenditure that affects GPMs, and every product purchase expenditure does, you have to generate higher margin sales and/or adjust your *cost of goods sold* (COGS), to maintain or improve your GPMs.

Don't feel defensive if your GPMs go down, when you desire to have them go up. It's easy to lose sight of GPMs if you are not monitoring them constantly, and it's easy to have expenses creep up on you.

But from an acquirer's perspective, slippage in GPMs is viewed as you essentially leaving money on the table. Here's why. If you have a 30% GPM on $100 million in sales, you're booking $30,000,000 gross margin with your existing company infrastructure (product mix, staff, pricing systems, inventory, etc.) If you slip to 27%, then your gross profit drops to $27,000,000. That's $3,000,000 less than the previous year, yet you were delivering essentially the same service with the same staff. An acquirer will look at that $3,000,000 as money that you could have realized with more aggressive cost or pricing management.

Let's say your GPMs go up from 27% to 28%, yet were at 30% two years ago. From an acquirer's point of view, that 1% increase (year-over-year, from 27% to 28%) will not be viewed as a raging success, even though you increased gross profit by $1,000,000. Instead, the acquirer will likely ask why you can't get back to and maintain the 30% gross margin you had two years earlier.

Now, let's say that you have a three-year track record of increasing GPMs each year for the past three or four years.

Now that's progress!

If your business climbs from 27%, to 28% to 29% to 30%, you are obviously controlling your COGS, and improving the selling margin of your product mix. In this scenario, for a $100 million operation, your gross profit climbed from $27,000,000 to $30,000,000, as you were able to wring out purchasing inefficiencies, increased direct labor productivity, took advantage of prepay discounts from suppliers, and optimized your product/customer mix, yet still deliver the quality products and services to your customer base.

Now here's the example that really put a cherry on top. Let's say that the GPMs for your business climb from 27%, to 28% to 29% to 30%, and your revenue is climbing as well, say, from $100 million to $108 million over this period of time. Acquirers will swoon over a company that shows year-over-year sales growth and improved GPMs. It shows you're growth-focused and disciplined over costs of goods and pricing… *and* that you've optimized the blend of customers with a bias toward higher-margin sales. That's a business that will get the highest value in any economy.

> *"Don't be distracted by criticism. Remember—the only taste of success some people get is to take a bite out of you."*
>
> *– Zig Ziglar*

Chapter 12

Maximize Business Value with Credits to EBITDA

EBITDA, a GAAP financial measure, is a key component in the valuation of your business. The reason is simple: EBITDA is used as a proxy for operating cash flow. However, often overlooked in the sale of a business are the adjustments you can make to your earnings, a.k.a. *Adjusted EBITDA* (a Non-GAAP financial measure) that can have a significant impact on business valuation.

For example, a typical valuation multiple is 7X EBITDA, so a company booking $3 million in EBITDA would sell for $21 million. But let's say you found $300,000 to credit to your *adjusted EBITDA*. That would boost the business value by $2.1 million dollars. So, it's worth taking a good long look at possible credits.

Keep in mind that credits to EBITDA are typically one-time expenses that occur during your fiscal year (or calendar financial accounting year) and which *won't repeat* in the future or after the sale of your business.

As a rule, buyers will closely scrutinize each adjustment to EBITDA, so credits must be legitimate and agreed upon with the buyer. (A word of caution: Don't nickel and dime the adjustments. Adjustments to EBITDA of less than $1,000 should probably not be considered; they are often called "ash and trash.")

To determine what adjustments are typical, consult with your investment banker about what constitutes an adjustment to EBITDA, but here are some typical examples:

- **Owner salaries and bonuses**

As an owner, if your salary plus bonus is $300,000 per year, but the market rate to replace you is $200,000, you can most likely take a legitimate $100,000 adjustment to EBITDA. (Remember the economic value of a $100,000 adjustment is a $700,000 increase in company value!)

- **Rent of the facilities**

If the rent you are charging your business is below fair market value, the difference could be a negative adjustment to EBITDA. If the rent is above fair market value, that would be a positive adjustment to EBITDA, in favor of the buyer. It all depends on the terms of the lease.

- **Personal Owner Expenses**

For private businesses, it's common (though not always recommended by the IRS) for some owner's personal expenses to be credited to the business, e.g. a family member that is on the payroll, club memberships, or sports tickets that the acquirer would not pay post-acquisition. Those are likely EBITDA credits.

- **Non-recurring professional fees**

Valid credits to EBITDA include *one-time* legal fees or a settlement from a lawsuit, non-recurring consulting fees, and non-repeating marketing expenses that are attached to a specific marketing program.

- **Infrastructure, equipment, software, IT upgrade investments**

The key to recognizing these credits rests on whether the investment was expensed or capitalized, as opposed to a one-time expense. If it was expensed as a one-time expense, it may be eligible as an adjustment to EBITDA. If it was capitalized, then it is not eligible since it is on a depreciation schedule, which flows through your income statement. Keep in mind, you are already getting credit for your depreciation since EBITDA is earnings before interest, taxes, *depreciation*, and amortization. So, one-time expenses, if they are being amortized, would not qualify as an adjustment to EBITDA.

- **Other one-time expenses**

A note of caution: If your one-time expenses have recurred on your income statements in prior years (if not *last* year) and are projected to show up in future years (if not *next* year), they are simply not one-time expenses that can be used as adjustments to EBITDA.

Legitimate expenses vs. non-legitimate one-time expenses that can be used as an adjustment to EBITDA will be readily determined in discussion with your investment banker and your accountant. Be sure to have that discussion so that you don't leave money on the table. Adjustments to EBITDA are common, and it is an opportunity to increase the value of your business, sometimes dramatically. But it needs to be done carefully with one thought in mind: Will the buyer accept the adjustment to EBITDA as legitimate and fair?

"Always look for the fool in the deal.

If you don't find one, it's you."

— *Mark Cuban*

Chapter 13

What Are Earnouts? How Do They Work?

An "earnout" is commonly used in merger and acquisitions transactions. Essentially, an earnout is a risk-allocation provision, where part of the purchase price of a company is deferred and not paid in cash at closing. The earnout is paid out based on the performance of the acquired business over a specific period of time.

The reason earnouts are used is simple: They can bridge the gap between the seller, who wants the highest possible valuation, and the buyer, who may be willing to pay top dollar, but only if the business achieves a specified performance metrics usually based on gross revenue, sales revenue, net profit, or EBITDA, usually based on gross revenue, sales revenue, net profit, or EBITDA.

As discussed elsewhere in this book, when valuing a business, most buyers use data from the last fiscal year, while also examining financial statements that reach back three years or more. But what if the seller is well into the financial year at the time of sale, and he's putting up great numbers, with strong growth? The seller rightfully wants to get rewarded for that performance, which may not be reflected in the last fiscal year's financial reports. In this case, if the seller requests it, the buyers could consider pegging the company's value to the trailing twelve months (TTM) performance, which represents the last twelve months of results prior to the closing.

Ok, let's look at an example. Let's say that a seller wants to sell his business in the middle of the fiscal year. But, with sales on an upswing, he wants a valuation credit for the remainder of the budgeted year. Let's assume this business did $2 million in EBITDA the previous year, and is projected to do $2.3 million in EBITDA in the current year.

Based on a 7X multiple of EBITDA for both periods, the valuation for the previous year's performance would be $14 million. Now, apply the same multiple to the current year, and the valuation rises to $16.1 million. In this scenario, the buyer agrees to the valuation of $14 million based on the previous year's results. The seller is paid $14 million in cash at closing. But the seller doesn't want to leave any money on the table, since he's having a good year. So, for the current year, the buyer and seller agree to a $2.1 million earnout. The earnout will be paid *if* the seller achieves $2.3 million in EBITDA for current year.

When structuring the performance metrics for an earnout, be exceedingly careful and seek advice from an experienced investment banker. As a seller, you want to use fair financial metrics that you can achieve and be able to manage operations you still control after the initial deal has closed. The buyer is typically interested in one financial target: the bottom line, either net income or EBITDA. No matter what metrics are chosen to peg to the earnout, what's really important is that the terms are fully and easily understood, and are perceived as fair by both sides.

Let's look at the seller and the buyer's perspective: The seller needs to be clear about what the buyer will control, *post close*. At a minimum, the seller will want to protect the resources necessary to achieve his earnout targets. But if the buyer is going to tack on additional costs to the seller's business, such as expenses for selling, or general and administrative (SG&A) expenses, then the seller should probably avoid pegging the earnout to EBITDA.

When determining targets for that scenario, consider tying the earnout to sales or gross profit dollars instead of EBITDA. If the buyer agrees that no additional SG&A costs will be added to the business—post close and during the earnout period—then EBITDA can be considered. In any event, a clear understanding of the terms and metrics is essential to keep both sides happy, cooperative, and working together toward their mutual success.

A final note: We are often approached by sellers and they ask, "Just ballpark, what multiple of value can you get in today's market?"

Let's say that the market rate for cannabis and hemp companies is 7X for all-cash-at-close transactions. If the seller making the inquiry is shopping around for an investment banker / M&A advisory firm, they will sometimes say: *"Well, I've got another firm that says they can get me 12X."* We often respond: "Well, you should go with them because we think that is unrealistic in today's market."

What has likely happened is that seller has confused the multiple that can be obtained in an all-cash-at-close deal, with the higher multiple that might be paid in a multi-year earnout. To be clear, it is often the case that if the seller wants to share risk with the acquirer, and stretch his earnout payments out for multiple years, then a higher multiple can be obtained. In the calculus, be sure that you understand what the multiple would be for a *cash deal*, as opposed to a deal where the acquirer pays just a little up front, and you, the seller, go along for the nail-biting ride as you share in the ups and down of the business cast out over multiple years. More risk, more potential reward. But there's nothing like the security of a cash-at-close transaction.

"It's hard to do a really good job on anything you don't think about in the shower."

—Paul Graham

Chapter 14

Earnings Quality and the Buyer's Right to Know

Everyone wants to sell their business at peak earnings. Who wouldn't? Since most businesses are purchased as a multiple of earnings, you as a seller have substantial motivation to get those earnings as high as possible (on a trailing-12-month basis or previous-fiscal-year/calendar-year basis) before you put your company up for sale. Every dollar added to EBITDA can bring back a substantial return in valuation, often 5X, 6X, or even 7X.

Most prospective buyers expect to see this pattern of selling on an uptick. It's only natural; indeed, any business that tries to sell at a low point in the business cycle would be looked upon with suspicion, and accordingly, it would receive a poor valuation.

But buyers considering purchasing companies, which are selling at a time of peak earnings have the right to question two things: the *quality* of those earnings and the *sustainability* of those earnings in the future.

Quality of the Earnings

The quality of the earnings is an indication of how likely they are to continue. High-quality earnings don't necessarily have to show up on your books as repeat business, although that is certainly desirable, since repeat business costs the least to acquire.

But high-quality can also mean consistent earning levels or consistent rates of increases year to year, whether the source is repeat business or new business. High-quality earnings point to a quality sales staff and a disciplined company that works hard to take care of its customers.

Let's look at an example. Say a business shows sales of $25 million three years ago, $27 million two years ago, $29 million last year, and a prediction of $31 million this year. Let's also say that the company has consistently shown 10% EBITDA margins, with an unadjusted EBITDA of $2.5MM, $2.7MM, and $2.9MM respectively, and a projected $3.1MM this year.

A prospective buyer looking at that company will have no problem believing the current fiscal year's projections, even with just a few months of data to go on, because the earnings have shown consistent high-quality growth.

If another business were to show jagged sales and EBITDA margins that bounce around year for year, with no symmetry, followed by a killer year of strong sales and high EBITDA margins, the potential buyer isn't going to have a great deal of faith in a recent, spectacular 12-month period. That's because the recent numbers may not represent a trend that will continue. In fact, they are likely to represent a "sugar high" that can't be consistently replicated. Red flags will pop up on the deal, and valuation won't be based in the trailing twelve months, but perhaps on earnings *averaged out* over the past three years.

Sustainability of Earnings

Simply put, the sustainability of earnings indicates the likelihood that current earnings will continue to grow / keep pace at roughly the same rate as the *cost of goods sold* (COGS) expenditure levels.

It's even more impressive if you can show that you can sustain or increase your earnings while *lowering* COGS over time, indicating that you are always working to drive up efficiency.

If you had a great year, but you know in your heart that you will have to increase marketing costs and salesforce salaries the following year to retain those customers, then the sustainability of the earnings is lower, and your customer retention may be more volatile than current earnings indicate.

The same principle holds for a seller who positions his/her company for sale by making an effort to suppress COGS. Some examples include: deferring necessary maintenance, not filling a position that needs to be filled, or misallocating expenses into a different time period than the allocation of earnings, just to obtain an earnings credit that really should be an expense.

A prudent buyer will examine your COGS along with your maintenance schedules, and historical staffing levels / future staffing needs to see how they have changed over time with respect to your earnings.

Finally, if you reported earnings that you have yet to collect, (e.g. pending AR) and you are using an accrual accounting basis, you will have credited those to EBITDA. But the prospective buyer will be within his/her rights to question whether those reflect accurate earnings, especially if there is a history of bad pays that have not properly been accounted for in your bad debt allowances.

No Tricks

There is no trick to reporting the quality and sustainability of earnings. It's about divulging what's fair and reasonable, properly allocating earnings and expenses, and forthrightly calculating COGS in a way that buyer and seller agree is accurate.

"There is only one boss. The customer. And he can fire everybody in the company from the chairman on down, simply by spending his money somewhere else."

— Sam Walton

Chapter 15

How Much Cash Must You Leave Behind?

In every acquisition, there is one common question that the seller asks as the deal moves toward closing: *How much cash will I be required to leave in the business?*

Obviously, sellers don't want to leave "too much" cash or cash equivalents in the coffers. At the same time, the buyer wants to ensure they have enough cash to run the business, because *the last thing* an acquirer wants to do is put cash into a business soon after buying it.

Make no mistake: From the buyer's perspective, inheriting a big fat balance of cash or cash equivalents is a plus. But you, the seller, are not required to leave over-large balances for the new owner. Obviously, there is a balance to be struck between buyer and seller.

But what's fair? What formula can be used that's acceptable to all, a formula that won't start a battle or create a sticking point as you move toward closing the deal?

Luckily, there is a tried-and-true formula for calculating an acceptable cash or cash equivalent balance to be left in place for the new owner. This *working capital ratio* is widely used, and we have never seen meaningful pushback on it, as long as there aren't extraordinary liabilities to cover, which are the seller's responsibility.

The typical acceptable working capital ratio is 1.5 to 1. (That ratio works for *most* types of businesses, recognizing that each business type will can have its idiosyncrasies, and that's especially true of businesses that carry inventory or that deal with inventory turns.) As for that 1.5 to 1 ratio, when you sell your business, you should leave $1.50 in current assets on hand for every $1 in current liability. Before handing over your business, anything over that amount can be likely withdrawn by you, the seller, without raising protests from the buyer. (Extract this cash substantially before you close the deal so it doesn't look like a last-minute grab, which could raise red flags.)

Here's an example of how to calculate that figure. Your current assets are typically represented by three categories: *Cash on Hand*, *AR*, and *Inventory* (if you maintain any).

Your current liabilities are typically AP and other payable liabilities, including pre-pays for items or services you have not yet delivered.

Let's plug in some numbers and calculate an actual ratio.

Assume you have the following current assets:

- Cash: $1,500,000
- AR: $300,000

- Inventory: $50,000

Your total current assets are $1,850,000.

(Pro-Tip: When calculating the AR figure, be sure to account for any bad debt that you might experience. If you historically collect 96% of your AR, don't make an assumption of 100% when calculating the working capital ratio. You would likely be called out on that by the acquirer and asked to correct it.)

Now let's look at current liabilities.

Assume you have the follow current liabilities:

- AP: $500,000
- Other: $50,000

Your total current liabilities are $550,000.

Now let's express that as a ratio by dividing the current assets by the current liabilities.

The formula would look like this: $1,850,000 / $550,000 = 3.3 to 1.

In this case, a business owner with $1,850,000 in current assets and $550,000 in current liabilities has a 3.3:1 *Working Capital Ratio* ("WCR"), *far more* than what an acquirer can reasonably expect to be left in the business upon an acquisition.

Since current assets exceed liabilities, you (the seller) can work your current assets down, typically by extracting cash. You would take enough out so that you achieve a 1.5 to 1 ratio at the time of sale.

In this case, we would advise the owner who is selling the business to work current assets down to $825,000. (We achieved that $825,000 figure by simply multiplying the liabilities by 1.5. The formula looks like this: $550,000 x 1.5 = $825,000.) That ratio works very much in favor of the owner who is selling. He or she can work the current assets of $1,850,000 down to $825,000 by extracting $1,025,000 *or* the acquirer would have to come up with that figure upon close.

Will an acquirer scream and shout when he realizes that you are taking cash out of the business ahead of a sale? Not if you make the case for a reasonable working capital ratio, and use the industry standard 1.5:1 number in your calculation.

> *"Perfection is not attainable,
> but if we chase perfection we
> can catch excellence."*
>
> *– Vince Lombardi*

Chapter 16

The (Irksome) Due Diligence Process

The excitement of receiving a *letter of intent* (LOI) for your business is something all sellers look forward to. The LOI maps out the price a buyer will pay, the terms and timing of the payment, and—if your investment banker has done a good job—important specifics, such as how the working capital "peg" will be calculated. When the LOI is finally negotiated, agreed to, and signed by all parties, the due diligence process begins. The due diligence process is designed to give the buyer a chance to:

1. Verify everything that was stated in the *Informational Memorandum.*
2. Process a long list of clearances and legal issues that need to be resolved before the sale can move to close.

Make no mistake, the due diligence process is time-consuming, and it often distracts the most important people in the business with information retrieval and financial reporting tasks. Before we get into a sampling of what the due diligence process entails, keep one thing in mind. This time-consuming nature of the process presents a unique problem for the seller. Here's why: The due diligence process can take upwards of three to four months for a even small-sized deals. During that time, your company has to hit the financial performance that was predicted in the *Informational Memorandum.* If you miss those numbers, the buyer has the right to reexamine the deal and potentially "re-price" their offer based on the new numbers. (The buyers will almost never go higher if you beat your predictions, but they often go lower if you miss them.)

Unfortunately, the people needed to make those numbers are often the very people most involved with, and most distracted by, the due diligence process. So, time management and multi-tasking are the watchwords of success here. This is especially true for the CEO, COO, and the CFO (as well as the bookkeepers and your accounting firm).

When the due diligence list comes over from the buyer (typically in a spreadsheet), be sure you're *sitting down* when you open it. This will lower your risk of injury when you faint. The list is often *a dozen or more pages long*, and can have 200 line items for your team to address. Each line item is a request for information. Here's a sample look at the level of detail that is often required in the due diligence process.

- **HR and Benefits**

A full accounting of every employee's earnings, commissions, bonuses, last raises, and benefits (including 401k plans, and raise / bonus policies), including their hire dates and duration of employment.

- **IT**

All software licenses will need to be current, at your expense; descriptions of security, backup, disaster recovery, and extra capacity plans for databases, as well as all vendor contacts.

- **Security**

"Anyone who touches money" will be subject to a thorough background check, and required to sign a waiver allowing the research to be done.

- **Safety**

Many buyers acquiring a workplace, such as a lab, distribution center, or warehouse, may be implementing new safety protocols, and they will want a thorough review of what you have in place already.

- **Customer interviews**

All buyers will want to interview a sampling of customers. Requests for 100 names are not unusual.

- **Regulatory compliance**

In the cannabis and hemp sectors, regulatory compliance is key, and the due diligence process will often require the presentation of proof of compliance. If you are operating equipment, calibration statements may be required.

- **Site visits and environmental inspection**

Got a toxic spill on your site? A buried tank? This part of the process will ferret all of that out, typically using an Environmental Site Assessment (ESA) test.

We've listed just seven possibilities of what might be 200 request categories. And we haven't even gotten into the financial reporting required, e.g. trial balances, balance sheets and P&L by division (all to be supplied *each month* during due diligence), receivables aging, inventory and inventory reserve balances, etc. The list really does go on and on.

Ready to handle that, as you run a successful business?

The companies that handle this process well are the ones that exclusively charge an employee or two with the task of rounding up the material and dogging the information and data. You can't complete the process by paying attention to it for a few minutes each day.

DropBox is a superb tool for managing the process. Secure access to DropBox can be granted to multiple parties, and folders and sub-folders can be set up for each line item, so your compliance / progress can be readily checked and tracked. Email alerts can let all parties know every time a folder is changed or a file is added or edited. Also, with DropBox, you won't be emailing files and wrestling with version control as information is edited and updated.

The relief felt when the due diligence process is completed is *almost* better than the thrill of seeing funds wired to you at closing. Almost.

> *"If one does not know to which port one is sailing, no wind is favorable."*
>
> — *Lucius Annaeus Seneca*

Chapter 17

Are You Too Ready to Sell?

We often get inquiries from business owners who start the conversation this way: "Well," (deep sigh of relief) "I'm finally ready to sell."

But all too often, they are too ready to sell. That's because the owner has decided not just to sell, but to fully retire as soon as possible, with no intentions to stay on to manage the business post-acquisition. That owner wants to hand over the keys, take the check to the bank, and maybe work on his or her sailing skills.

Unfortunately, as attractive as it may be for an owner to dust off their hands and walk away, that quick exit is highly frowned upon by acquiring companies. Worse, it can cost the departing owner millions of dollars in lost valuation.

Here's why: Most acquiring companies want business and leadership continuity. They want to keep the leaders (indeed, the whole team) in place that made the company so successful. Most acquiring companies want at least a year of post-acquisition service from the departing owner, ideally more.

If the owner says they're "out the door," that can easily knock the price of a company down a "turn" or two (2x), if not more. In other words, if the company would have been purchased at a 6x multiple of EBITDA, the deal might sink to 5X EBITDA. If the EBITDA is $1,000,000, the company won't sell for $6,000,000, but for $5,000,000 instead. Here's another way to look at that: If the departing owner were told that he or she would be given $1,000,000 to *stay* for an *additional* year (more than $19,000/week!), she or he would probably jump at the chance, because, well, that's a lot of juice. Yet when that same departing owner insists on leaving the company immediately upon an acquisition, he may not have the perspective to see how much money he is leaving on the table with a lower valuation.

Prepare with Replacement Personnel

If you are an owner, and you want to leave as soon as your company is acquired, why not take the prudent step of replacing yourself a year in advance of the sale?

That takes some real patience and planning; make no mistake. But the planning ahead may prevent an owner from making an impulse call to an investment banker to say, "I'm finally ready to sell." Plus, as an added benefit to the valuation equation, the departing owner's salary, benefits, and related costs can often be credited to the EBITDA, since it is not going to be a recurring future cost.

Now, how do you install a replacement for yourself? No matter what your title— president, CEO, or COO —if you can't promote talent from within, bring in a top-notch executive recruiter, and get your replacement installed at least 12 months before you pull the trigger on a sale.

When searching for your replacement, be completely transparent about your plans. Inform the incoming executive that he or she is there to take over in a transition that includes a planned change of ownership. (Note that acquiring companies often put incentives and equity in place for senior executives as a retention strategy, which can be a bonus for the incoming talent.) An ambitious replacement executive will see a real chance to prove his or her worth, and he or she can have a year ramp-up to make their mark.

With the replacement in place, the outgoing owner can ease out of operations and serve as a senior advisor, a role he or she may want to continue to play in the year(s) after an acquisition as well. As for the acquiring company, it will likely not view the departure of the owner as a high-impact loss, because so much preparation has been made to replace his or her talents and fill the roles he or she played.

Finally, this preparation pays well. With the right executive in place, and the outgoing owner's transition so well managed, think of how much company value will have been protected and preserved. It is far more than the all-in costs of the new hire, to say nothing of what this leadership continuity does to ensure a smooth transition of ownership for all of the employees.

"The secret to success is to know something nobody else knows."

– Aristotle Onassis

Chapter 18

Asset Sale or Stock Sale?

One common question that comes up as a deal moves toward a closing is whether the sale should be an asset sale or a stock sale.

A couple of quick points before we get into specifics: First, this chapter contains around 1/100th the information required to adequately cover this topic. So, any decision you make— asset vs. stock— must be made in consultation with your accountant and tax attorney. Second, in the "lower middle market" (up to $100 million in sales), 70%+ of sales are asset sales, because, to put it bluntly, that's what buyers demand.

Of the five different company types, (sole proprietorships, LLCs, partnerships, C-corporations and sub-S corporations), each has idiosyncrasies that will affect your election. However, "non-corporate entities" (sole proprietorships, LLCs, and partnerships) can present a special tax peril for the sellers, and no one-size-fits-all rule applies. In the most general terms, the election to go with an asset sale or a stock sale largely depends on the legal liability assumed by the acquirer, and by the tax implications to the seller and acquirer.

Liabilities. In an asset sale, the acquirer gets to rule in and rule out what assets it wants to purchase, whereas in a stock sale the liabilities are not just the encumbrances of the assets, but also any liability that may arise for wrongdoing of the entity under its prior ownership… unless the seller rules out certain liabilities in the "representations and warranties" within the purchase agreement.

(See why most acquirers want an asset sale?)

Depreciation. In an asset sale, the acquirer's basis for depreciation is the fair value paid for each asset, or class of assets, regardless of the tax basis of each asset or all assets taken aggregately. To the extent that the fair value of the company is greater than the fair value of its assets, this "excess" is allocated to "goodwill," which is depreciated for tax purposes as a separate asset over 15 years. So, the acquirer has an incentive to allocate as much of the purchase price as possible to assets with the shortest recovery periods, determined with reference to the allocable purchase price. The seller's gain is determined with reference to the basis in each asset sold rather than the aggregate basis of all assets.

(Again, you see why acquirers want an asset sale.)

Rights: In a stock sale, there may be a risk of minority stock holders blocking a sale. Many corporations protect minority shareholder rights by agreement, but such agreements can also compel minority shareholders to sell their interests, even when they don't agree with the majority. This a frequent occurrence. Indeed, minority shareholders may even assert their rights by filing a lawsuit claiming that majority shareholders are betraying fiduciary duties.

Assets. Note that in an asset sale, there are some assets that are difficult for a seller to assign to an acquirer, such as certain agreements struck by the company, or a land-use covenant assigned to the seller's family; or licenses, or permits… the list goes on. A stock sale entitles the acquirer to these assets without a reassignment, driving down legal costs and the time it takes to close a deal.

Taxes. Generally, the taxes are higher for the seller in an asset sale because of the differential tax rates that may apply to certain types of assets. The seller may end up paying capital gains rate on some aspects of the sale, and the seller's marginal rate on others. Note that the seller's tax treatment is due to tax rates on certain types of assets, but also due to exposure to ordinary income treatment for the portion of gain attributable to recapture of prior depreciation.

What's Right for You?

Confused? We don't blame you. When I'm asked if a stock sale or an asset sale is preferred, I say, "well, it depends, but the best advice I can offer is to speak with your tax accountant and a solid tax attorney."

Every business is idiosyncratic. When determining what's best, we look at tax implications, the number of share-holders, and how willing they all are to sell their shares. We also look at the company's locations, as well as the nature of the assets themselves (e.g. are there an abundance of licenses, permits, leases, etc.?), and all potential liabilities – the known knowns and unknown unknowns. Only then do we make a recommendation that's right for our client.

"If you are willing to do more than you are paid to do, eventually you will be paid to do more than you do."

– Anonymous

Chapter 19

Leave Profanity and Politics at the Door

Deals go south and suitors bow out of contention for lots of reasons, typically lack of strategic fit, inadequate cash flow, or because the deal is offered at the wrong time in the business cycle.

Or at least that's what departing suitors will *say* are the reasons for backing away… But it's not uncommon for a suitor to back away because of a cultural or personality mismatch.

Politics. If politics get brought up for discussion, avoid it. As a seller, you can't predict politics of the suitor. Don't make an assumption that they'll agree with your point of view, liberal or conservative. If you voice strong political opinions, and the suitor disagrees with your politics, they probably won't mention it out of politeness. But as soon as the they get in the airport car, they may very well dismiss the deal as impossible due to a potential mismatch of values. Even if they happen to agree with you, your political views will have very little bearing on the value of your company. So why risk bringing it up? It's universally safe to keep political discussions out of the mergers and acquisitions process.

Profanity. We have been around the block a couple times, so salty language is nothing new to us. And we're not naïve. We recognize that people who work together over a long period of time can probably let a profane word slip without unduly offending those around them. But you cannot assume that it's appropriate to speak profanely in front of people you meet in the deal-vetting process. You simply can't predict how they will respond.

We have never seen someone give an encouraging look when someone they've just met speaks profanely. Yet we *have* heard people, as they walk away from a meeting, say, "I have to say, I'm just not comfortable with that language. Can you imagine if they said that around *our* office?"

Whether you're an altar boy or a sailor, *zip it,* when you're tempted to spout off in meetings with potential acquirers.

Libations. Business dinners very often involve a cocktail, beer, or a nice bottle of wine, but – especially on the "first date" between a suitor and a seller – a drink or two is probably more than enough to put people at ease, and open up for some bonding conversations. Any excess drinking during meet-and-greets is universally looked upon as a negative in a business deal. Even the perception of excess drinking is a *no no…* Your nightly standard 3rd glass of wine may seem to a suitor as flat-out excess. And if the acquirer's team doesn't order any libations, consider skipping it yourself. Most suitors will likely look upon a seller's excesses around libations, and think, "I'm just not doing a business deal with a person who drinks like that." Save the all-night toasts for when the deal is done, and you're just among old friends.

Sports. Unless you can all agree to the unspoken truth that Tom Brady is the best quarterback that has ever played football (because, you must admit, he is), it's best to avoid sports, *at first*. Sports can be a great bonding experience with strangers, but sense them out first before making blanket pronouncements like the one we just made about the great Tom Brady, the greatest of all time.

Religion and Ethnic Identification. Here's another area where it's surprised us more than once when a seller makes a comment about a religious or ethnic group. Not only will a suitor's antenna go up around potential discrimination lawsuits and other liabilities, but it's just bad form to imply that you focus on cultural differences inspired by religious or ethnic groups. Keep those discussions to yourself.

Is everyone a perfect gentleman or lady? No, and we're the first to admit to imperfections. But the topics listed above are ones where you should steer clear of controversy, lest you bring about judgement by someone who might otherwise be willing to write you a nice check.

"Chains of habit are too light to be felt, until they are too heavy to be broken."

—*Warren Buffett*

Chapter 20

"Pricing In" a Recession

You can't go long in any economy before you start to hear talk of a recession. That's true whether it's 2020, 2010, 2000, or 1990. All day long, you'll hear predictions from economists about what the future holds. One will say there's a recession coming; the next one will say we're set for growth, and the third will say it will be a flat year. (You may even see predictions that the price of tomatoes will rise, but ignore that. That's because business owners are buying up the tomatoes to throw at the economists.)

No matter what the fate of the economy, in the world of mergers and acquisitions, you can rest assured that prospective buyers of your cannabis or hemp company will try to leverage economic uncertainty and recessionary storm clouds to offer less for your company than they would in a time of economic growth.

That should not come as a surprise.

There is always a natural tension between sellers (the optimists) who want the highest imaginable valuation, and buyers (the pessimists, *at least temporarily*) who want to drive the valuation lower.

That said, exactly how would acquirers drive down the value of your company to *price in* or *guard against* a potential recession. They will do this in at least two ways: 1) Offering a lower multiple paid for your company, and 2) the implementation of earnouts.

First, as background, let's review a topic covered elsewhere in this book. If you are selling a company with a $3 million EBITDA, and it's valued at 5.5X, your company value is $16.5 million. However, if there are recessionary clouds on the horizon, the buyer will likely *price in* the potential slowdown by lowering the multiple he or she is willing to pay. Just dropping the multiple from 5.5X to 5X will lower the purchase price by $1.5 million. As you see, even a "half turn down" – just a slight softening – can have a dramatic and negative effect on value. So, in a recession, or even in the face of a *prospective* recession, a buyer may simply offer a lower multiple for your company in *anticipation* of a downturn.

A second technique for pricing in a recession in an earnout. An earn-out is a risk-allocation vehicle that can bridge the gap in value between the buyer and the seller. Essentially, with an earn out (as spelled out in the definitive purchase agreement), a portion of the purchase price for the company is deferred. The earn-out, which is typically a relatively small percentage of the overall deal value, is paid over a specific period of time, post-closing, based on the performance of the acquired business.

Essentially, the buyer says: *I think the market will soften, so I want to pay less.* The seller says: *I think the market will be strong, so I want you to pay more.*

The earnout can bridge the gap, essentially saying: *Hey folks, let's put a mechanism in place that will reward the correct party a year from now, or two years from now, when we'll see who's right.*

The earnout approach will work only if the seller agrees to peg a future payout to certain performance metrics. If the metrics are achieved, the seller gets the earnout; if the seller misses the mark, he or she won't get the earnout (or gets only a fraction of it).

For example, in the simplest terms, assuming a $3 EBITDA, you may get 5X at close and receive $15 million. Then, an additional 0.5X is paid a year after close ($1.5 million more), *if* you perform.

Earnout structures can be remarkably creative, and they are can based on all (or some) of a range of performance metrics, such as gross revenue, sales revenue, net profit, or EBITDA. When structuring them, here's *a word to the wise*, as covered earlier: Some buyers will want earnouts to be "all-or-none." If the seller agrees to, say, achieve $20 million in revenue, the buyer may want to pay out *zero dollars* if the seller comes in at $19.9 million. So, when structuring an earnout, drive to make it *graduated*, not all-or-none.

If you achieve 80% of your goal, you should get 80% of the earnout. If you reach 90%, you get 90%.

Earnouts can also be structured to reward you if you *exceed* the amount targeted in the earnout. Say you knock it out of the park in the year of the sale and achieve 110% of your earnout target. You should be rewarded for that extra performance. If you're a seller, and you have a good investment banker advising you, he or she should be putting these ideas in front of you and driving to have them accepted by the buyer.

Finally make sure to maintain control of your operations. If the earnout is based on an EBITDA performance metric, and the acquirer layers in corporate overhead, you have just lost some control of your EBITDA. Protections against this and similar occurrences can be built into a deal structure by a good advisor.

"Don't worry about people stealing your design work.

Worry about the day they stop."

—*Jeffrey Zeldman*

Chapter 21

Can Your Company be Re-Priced After the LOI?

Here's a dreadful prospect that you want to avoid. Let's say that you put your company on the market, and – for ease of math – you are putting up good numbers at the time of sale, say, $2 million in EBITDA.

Your investment banker (broker) sends the deal teaser out to prospects, you get some interested parties, and someone comes in with a Letter of Intent (LOI) that offers a nice price. Say they offer today's going multiple of 5.5X adjusted EBITDA. In this case, the offer would be $11 million.

You like the price, so you turn away the other suitors, and agree to enter into the due diligence process and move toward a closing.

The Letter of Intent will often have a clause in the document that cites your projections for the amount of EBITDA you expect to book between the acceptance of the Letter of Intent and the closing date. To maintain that $2 million EBITDA pace, you have to continue to put around $183,000 in EBITDA each month on the bottom line.

Now what? Well, unfortunately, the due diligence process takes months. During that time, you're substantially distracted (as we've written about elsewhere in this book) with a boatload of requests for information…information that you never dreamed someone would ever want to know, e.g. environment assessment of your various real estate locations, introductions to customers for interviews…the list goes on and on. In fact, you're so distracted by the due diligence process that you miss your numbers, and you don't earn $183,000 in EBITDA two months before closing. In fact, you miss your number by $20,000. Then, the month before closing, you miss your numbers again, slipping $25,000 below the $183,000 projection.

These slippages off the pace of EBITDA are all reported to the prospective buyer on a monthly basis. That first month you miss your numbers, the buyers may have a few raised eyebrows, and they might even voice some mild concern. But that second month that you slip off the pace is trouble. The buyer may look at the two months as a trend, a downward trend… And they will surely vocalize their concern. The call starts out friendly, and goes something like this:

"Joe, I can't help but notice that you are not making your numbers. Any reason for that? I have to say that we are having some concerns…"

Joe say, "Well, heck Bob, I've been so distracted by all of your requests that I have not had time to focus on managing my sales team. Plus, I have not been able to make the calls that I typically make each month for our biggest customers."

Bob says, "Is your business so unstable and your profits so fragile that a few hours of your time each week can cause the business to tank? I think we have to reprice the deal."

Reprice the deal?! That is a phrase that has sent many a seller to the medicine cabinet, scrambling for his heart pills, following by an equally concerned investment banker who is trying to find out exactly how serious the buyer is about repricing.

Now let's look at a couple more points before we look at the math of how a buyer would reprice.

During due diligence, the acquirer will spend a lot of time with management understanding the relationship the target company has with its customers. The acquirer will look at the likelihood that customers will continue to buy through the company, post-close. At the last stage of the due diligence process, the acquirer will speak with the key customers or do a 3rd party satisfaction survey about the company. If the acquirer ascertains through these customer calls and surveys that some customers could be at risk post-close, repricing the deal could come into play.

Finally, even if the company is hitting its sales and EBITDA targets during the due diligence process, if customers are lost during process, it can materially impact the performance of the company of a go-forward basis, and here too, repricing could come into the picture.

Now let's take a look at the math of repricing, which is simple and rather brutal. Since the acquirer is paying on a multiple of EBITDA (e.g. 5.5X), they will apply that same multiple to the new EBITDA, adjusted downward, and calculated over a 12-month period. The $2 million EBITDA that got you an $11 million valuation may drop to $1.7 million, dropping the purchase price from $11 million to $9.35 million. (Remember, every dollar you drop in EBITDA can have a negative implication, X 5.5.)

Ironically, if you exceed your projected numbers during the due diligence process, there is little chance the buyer will reprice upwards, to give you a higher valuation. But negative repricing is all too real.

The ultimate solution: Avoid distractions during the due diligence process; don't neglect sales, and bring on staff that you can delegate parts of the due diligence process to. There's nothing worse that working for years to prepare your business for sale, only to have a couple of months of bad performance knock a million dollars or more off your value.

"Success consists of going from failure to failure without loss of enthusiasm."

— Winston Churchill

Chapter 22

Why Do Deals Fall Apart?

Acquisitions do not get completed due to concerns originating from two general sources: From the seller's point of view, the business owner can be disenchanted with the terms of the deal or – much more likely – its value. From the acquirer's point of view, they might have buyer's remorse (between when the LOI is signed and the deal closes) if doubts are raised about the quality of the earnings and whether the *sustainability* of the earnings are realistic after the close.

Deal Value Too Low

Let's look at the seller first. Most sellers have a firm price in their minds for what they want for their business. They've often worked many years to build up the business, and they want that work compensated for before they hand over the keys. Fair enough. That said, just as when selling a house you've remodeled and worked on yourself for years, the seller often has an inflated view of the value of the property which the acquirer may not share. The acquirer is not arriving at their number emotionally. They are using dispassionate comps and mathematical modeling to determine the offer price. The acquirer is not factoring in the times the seller may have worked over the Christmas holiday, or missed the kid's ball games, or didn't take vacations.

This emotional component enters into the acquisition process especially when the seller first sees the opening bids. Some sellers take affront when the amount offered is substantially lower than what they had in mind. But the bid amount is something the seller shouldn't take personally. The acquirer has a natural incentive to bid low (perhaps eventually adjusting upwards, if persuaded). Moreover, as mentioned, the acquirer is not just pulling a figure out of thin air. They're using third party reports to determine their bid value, triangulating off known values paid for similar deals, calculating the value of future earnings, and estimating how likely the company is to grow. They may have boards of directors to answer to, and they are highly unlikely to pay a premium just because they have the money to do so; in fact, generally speaking, the richer the buyer, the *less* they will pay.

That said, sellers will sometimes just "walk the deal," and leave what may be an accurate estimate of the company's value on the table. Fair enough. It's their company; they're entitled to do with it as they please.

Terms Unacceptable

A second situation arises when the bid amount is acceptable by the seller, but then the acquirer lays out *terms* that are unacceptable.

Generally, this takes the form of earn outs (one-year or multi-year) that require the seller to assume to much of the acquirer's risk. Terms can be too onerous, e.g. revenue goals set at too aggressive levels, or there's a loss of control over marketing budgets and hiring that you, the seller, feel are needed to meet the earn out. Here too the seller may look over the terms, and simply say there is too much put at risk, and "walk the deal."

It's About Earnings

Among the acquirer's concerns, earnings are paramount. Let's say an acquirer submits an LOI, and the value and terms are acceptable. What the acquirer will watch for between the signing of the LOI and the closing of the deal (when the *definitive purchase agreement* is signed) is whether the earnings hit the targets put forth by the seller in their *Informational Memorandum*, and whether the projected earnings can be sustained after the close.

In the *Informational Memorandum* the seller will set revenue and earnings projections that they promise to hit during the due diligence process, which can last months. If there is slippage on those numbers, and forecasts are missed, the acquirer will look very harshly on that, and – depending on the severity of the miss – potentially reprice the deal, inevitably lowering the amount they are willing to pay.

Moreover, during the due diligence process, the acquirer might determine that something is amiss in the company's ability to *sustain* their earnings. For example, let's say the seller loses key sales people when they heard of the sale of the company, or key customers leave for a competitor. Here too, the acquirer may request a repricing, or even back out of the deal entirely. To avoid this situation, make sure the *Informational Memorandum* is as accurate and realistic as possible, and that you have the team firmly in place that will remain in at the helm after the closing. That's the best way to ensure that a deal that's agreed to in the LOI ends up "sticking," and you drive to the closing with strong momentum.

> *"Whether you think you can,*
> *or think you can't – you're right."*
>
> *— Henry Ford*

Chapter 23

How to Communicate News of a Sale

It's hard to keep secrets around the office if more than a couple people are "in the know" about goings on. So, when a few members of your team are aware the company is going up for sale, it's difficult to keep the news as privileged information known only to a few. This is especially true in highly regulated businesses like cannabis and hemp, when odd and highly technical questions may start being asked of the staff.

Typically, when a company is prepping for sale, just the owners know initially. But the owners quickly realize they have to "bring others inside," to get information crucial to the offering, such as financial statements, customer lists, machine calibration reports, and inventory, etc. That's information required to create the *Informational Memorandum*. After all, you don't need to have a Ph.D. to recognize that owners are preparing to sell, when they start asking for historical quality-of-earnings statements and customer concentrations for three years running. So, let's prepare messaging now.

Typically, the pattern of communication that we see in our M&A practice goes like this: At first, just the owners are aware of the sale. They engage an investment banker (the seller's broker), who will request baseline information, including historical financial statements and *trailing twelve months* statements as well. That part of the process is easy to keep secret.

The next phase gets more complicated, in terms of confidentiality, because more detailed information has to be extracted from your accounting software or other record keeping programs; here's where the requests are peculiar, e.g. obtaining all leases on property, all regulatory reports filed with the state or federal government, etc. It's this second phase where you'd create an inner circle of a few trusted team members. To prepare for the expansion of those "in the know," consider putting a two-track communications plan in place: one for the inner circle, and – just to be careful – prep a communications plan for the company at large, in case the story leaks. (There's nothing more destructive than gossip about a sale, and potentially unfounded rampant fears of layouts, that sends employees running off to seek work from your competition.)

For the inner circle, consider this message: You are "seeking outside investment, which might result in the outright sale of the company if the terms are right." Further, explain that "this search for an investor is being done to onboard more energized management, offer everyone more opportunity, and access capital for expansion." Make clear that you are selling from a position of strength and profit, and that the management and employees are the true value of the company, not the inventory or buildings or equipment. Underscore how essential the people are to preserving continuity and ensuring stability. Point out that acquirers almost *never* put millions into a company only to lay off employees and shrink the operation. Acquirers have an entrepreneurial bias for expansion.

As the preparation for sale proceeds, especially when you start getting site visits from prospective acquirers, you will find the need to bring more people into the inner circle, and by then, it's increasingly hard to contain the news of a sale. (You can just about hear the comments in the office after site visits from prospective buyers: "Did you see those suits walking around today? Are we for sale?")

So, for the employees at large, be well-prepared with a message to them too, which is essentially the same one you delivered to the inner circle: *We are seeking investment to grow, which many result in a sale, but the value of the company is in the employees. Any acquirer will be extremely eager to retain and reward our workers. This is an exciting time of opportunity.*

Take the time to draft these messages into written statements. But it's probably best *not* to email these kinds of statements, because they can be easily forwarded. Instead, present the statement verbally at a company meeting, and take questions. Explain the importance of confidentiality.

Know that competitors will feast on the news that you are for sale, and they might imply that the volatility around the sale will lead to a drop-off in service or inventory and employee flight. So, while prepping these internal messages, draft one for customers too. If news of the prospective sale leaks out, you'll have a message ready to share with them. Finally, consider telling key customers about a potential sale long before they might hear any rumors, just to assure those high-volume accounts that things are good now…but they're going to get even better.

"If you can't feed a team with two pizzas, it's too large."

— Jeff Bezos

Chapter 24

How Investment Bankers Get Paid for Brokering the Sale

Investment bankers that broker the sale of your company have a fairly standard schedule for retainers and success fees. But there are idiosyncrasies and potential pitfalls to watch for. So, let's take a close look.

The Retainer: Most investment bankers charge a retainer to prepare your company for sale, often around $50,000. The retainer pays for ongoing expenses to prepare the "deal book" a.k.a. *Informational Memorandum,* which is used to shop the deal to acquirers. But the retainer should be paid out monthly (e.g. $10,000/month), not all upfront.

In many cases (and the way our firm works) the entire retainer is *refunded* to you, the seller, in the event of a success transaction. If the success fee paid to the investment banker turns out to be $250,000, the first $50,000 is refunded to you when the deal closes.

Beware of any investment bank that asks for the entire retainer in advance. After paying it all out, you might find it hard to get the investment banker's attention after a few weeks times.

The retainer pays the investment banker for the substantial hours their staff puts into creating the IM, as well as subscription fees to the expensive databases that are used to develop target lists and obtain the very latest deal values for similar companies that have been recently sold.

Investment bankers will insist on a retainer not only to defray preparation costs, but to make sure sellers have "skin in the game." That way, a seller won't just cavalierly commission an IM (often 40+ pages of detailed company background, with complete financial analysis) only to take the IM and walk away, or represent the company themselves using the investment banker's work.

The Success Fee: In addition to the retainer, most investment bankers charge a success fee based on the percentage of the deal value. A 5% fee is typical.

Some sellers may ask for a cap on the cash value of the fee, which might make the fee, in the end, valued at less than 5% of the overall deal value. The capped fee amount depends on the total paid for the company, and it's more likely for an investment banker to agree to a cap if the deal size is substantially over $40 million in value. In that case a cap on the success fee of $2,000,000 might be viewed as reasonable. But note that the success fee can also be staged, paying, say, 5% of the first $30 million, and then a smaller percentage for between $30 and $50 million, etc. It's all negotiable. If the proceeds of a sale are paid out to the seller over time (an *earnout*), the success fee should be paid as you, the seller, are paid over time.

Beware the investment banker who asks for a "guaranteed success fee," no matter the deal size. A guaranteed success fee is often requested for smaller deals, with transaction values under $10 million. If an investment banker seeks, say, a guaranteed $400,000 fee on a deal worth about $4 million, he's really asking for a 10% success fee, *twice* what he would normally receive. A customer-focused investment banker will typically not ask for a guaranteed fee and is happy to share the risk of the sale with his client.

Is the Success Fee Worth It?

In most deals (and this has invariably been the case with our firm), the investment banker earns back more than his success fee *just with credits to EBITDA*, which the clients would have otherwise missed. In other words, in the investment banker's financial analysis, the banker finds non-recurring charges, inventory credits, working capital credits, or charges that can be credited under new ownership which, when multiplied by today's valuation multiples (e.g. between 5X and 7X), *more than* earn back what the seller pays in success fees. In that case, the seller is effectively accessing the full range of the investment banker's services at low-cost / no-cost, including the *Informational Memorandum*, financial analysis, deal valuation, management of the auction / letter-of-intent processes, as well assistance in drafting the definitive purchase agreement, reps and warranties, asset declaration, and closing processes, to say nothing of help through due diligence.

Although many companies balk at the 5% fee, make no mistake: Investment bankers offer a service that avoids common seller errors, maximizes the sale value of your company, avoids pitfalls, and perhaps most importantly, allows a seller to run his business without distraction (and without the *substantial* demands on his time) from the complicated acquisition process.

About the Authors

John D. Wagner is a Managing Director for 1stWest Mergers & Acquisitions. John started his work in M&A when he served as director of corporate communications and investor relations for BuildNet, where he helped roll up 12 supply chain and workflow software companies in an 18-month period and served as liaison to the SEC. He has authored many private placement memorandums, an S1 document, and served as an M&A advisor on dozens of deals reaching back to 1999. John is the author of 16 books and 2,500+ articles that have appeared in the *Wall Street Journal*, *New York Times*, NPR, *LA Times*, and many other outlets. John is also CEO of J Wagner Media, a leading marketing firm: WhatAboutWagner.com.

For more than 20 years, **Dr. Carl Craig** has brought business acumen and scientific expertise together to develop strong technically focused businesses. His primary experience surrounds analytical instruments, chemicals, reagents, laboratory measurement, and medical diagnostics. As managing Director for 1st West Mergers and Acquisitions, Carl has leveraged both business and technology to assist the young and rapidly expanding cannabis sectors find full value in their businesses.

About 1stWest Mergers & Acquisitions

With transactions (to date) exceeding $1 billion in deal value, 1stWest Mergers & Acquisitions is full-service, international investment banking and advisory firm that is focused on the lower middle-market of companies with sales of up to $100 million. Established by Founding Partner Ted Rieple, 1stWest has built a highly successful practice assisting owners and shareholders in selling their companies, acquiring businesses, or raising growth capital. With managing directors in the U.S., Europe, Mexico, Panama, Peru, Brazil, Argentina and Chile, 1stWest is uniquely positioned to serve its clients around the globe. Learn more: www.1stWestMA.com

Contact

John D. Wagner: (919) 796-9984; J.Wagner@1stWestMA.com

Carl Craig: (303) 810-9095; C.Craig@1stWestMA.com

Glossary of M&A Terms

Here is a list of common terms used in mergers and acquisition. These definitions, obtained through various web sources (all cited below), have been supplemented and added to by the author.

Acquisition: One company taking over controlling interest in another company.

Add-On Acquisition: A strategic acquisition fit for an existing platform/ portfolio company.

Adjusted Book Value: The value that results after one or more asset(s) or liability amounts are added, deleted, or changed from their respective financial statement amounts.

Assets: The property of a business which is defined in an asset purchase agreement, but which generally includes real estate, tangible personal property such as office equipment, manufacturing, automobiles and inventory, as well as intangible assets such as patents, copyrights and trademarks, and may include cash and securities.

Asset (Asset-Based) Approach: A general way of determining a value indication of a business, business ownership interest, or security by using one or more methods based on the value of the assets of that business net of liabilities.

Audited Financial Statements: Financial Statements that have been audited by a Certified Public Accountant in accordance with Generally Accepted Accounting Principles (GAAP).

Balance Sheet: A snapshot of a company's financial condition. Assets, liabilities and ownership equity are listed as of a specific date, such as the end of its Fiscal Year.

Basket: The minimum threshold that must be exceeded before an acquirer is entitled to receive any indemnification payment for losses caused by a seller's breach of representations and warranties.

Book Value: A determination of a company's balance sheet value by adding all current and fixed assets and then deducting all debts, other liabilities and the liquidation price of any preferred issues. (Book value per common share is determined by dividing the book value by the number of common shares outstanding.)

Business Broker: An individual (or company) that solicits and represents business owners that are considering selling their business and acts as an intermediary between sellers (business owners) and buyers. Related uses or terms – intermediary, investment banker. A business broker that represents a seller is often said to be a "sell side rep."

Business Enterprise: A commercial, industrial, service, or investment entity, or a combination thereof, pursuing an economic activity.

Business Valuation: The act or process of determining the value of a business enterprise or ownership interest therein.

Capitalization: A conversion of a single period stream of benefits into value.

Capitalization Factor: Any multiple or divisor used to convert anticipated benefits into value.

Capital Structure: The composition of the invested capital of a business enterprise; the mix of debt and equity financing.

Cash Flow: Cash that is generated over a period of time by an asset, group of assets, or business enterprise. It may be used in a general sense to encompass various levels of specifically defined cash flows.

Closing: The event when the required legal agreements (e.g., stock purchase agreement, asset purchase agreement or merger agreement) are implemented between the parties and shares or assets are exchanged for the consideration specified in the agreements.

Confidentiality Agreement: This is the same as a Non-Disclosure Agreement, see below.

Cost of Capital: The expected rate of return (discount rate) that the market requires in order to attract funds to a particular investment.

Covenant Not To Compete, a.k.a. *non-compete*: An agreement often signed by an employee or a selling shareholder whereby they agree not to work for competitor companies or form a new competitor business within a specified period after termination of employment or the closing of the acquisition. Also called a "Non-Competition Agreement".

Deal Value: The sum of the consideration paid by the acquirer for the equity stake in the target company (plus the value of the net debt in the target, where applicable).

Debt Financing: This is when a firm raises money for working capital or capital expenditures by selling bonds, bills, or notes to individual and/or institutional investors. In return for lending the money, the individuals or institutions become creditors and receive a promise to repay principal and interest on the debt.

Discount: A reduction in value or the act of reducing value.

Due Diligence: A process where a buyer inspects a potential investment. Often includes a detailed review of accounting history and practices, operating practices, customer and supplier references, management references and market reviews.

Earn-Out: A contractual provision stating that the seller of a business is to obtain additional future compensation based on the business achieving certain future financial goals.

EBITDA: A financial term that is a rough proxy for free cash flow. Formally defined as Earnings before Interest and Taxes plus Depreciation and Amortization.

Enterprise Value: Enterprise value (EV) (also called *Total Enterprise Value*, or TEV) is a financial metric representing the entire value of a company after taking into account both holders of debt and equity.

Equity Risk Premium: A rate of return in addition to a risk-free rate to compensate for investing in equity instruments because they have a higher degree of probable risk than risk-free instruments (a component of the cost of equity capital or equity discount rate).

Exit Plan: A strategy, planned or unplanned, to depart an existing situation. The creation of an overall strategy that prepares a business owner and his/her company for the time when that business owner is no longer involved in the operations of the company. Examples of unplanned exits include death, divorce, incapacity, disability, management disputes, influx of competition, technological obsolescence, loss of a major customer, or other unforeseen economic events.

Exit: This occurs when a financial institution, such as private equity firm or venture capitalist realizes its investment in a company. This is usually achieved by selling its stake or by offering the company on the stock exchange.

Exit Multiples:

- Revenue multiple: Enterprise Value / Revenue
- EBITDA multiple: Enterprise Value / EBITDA
- Book Value multiple: Implied Equity Value / Book Value

Family Succession: In family successions or retirement transitions, ownership transfers from passive owners to active family members or outside shareholders. Facilitators are particularly sensitive to estate planning issues, family business dynamics, and the need for discretion and trust to make these transactions seamless and successful.

Fiscal Year: Typically a 12-month period over which a company budgets its spending.

Forced Liquidation Value: Liquidation value at which the asset or assets are sold as quickly as possible, such as at an auction.

Free Cash Flow: The cash generated by a business on a pre-tax, pre-interest basis after making positive adjustments for non-cash expenses such as depreciation and amortization as well as owner-related benefits and negative adjustments for capital expenditures.

GAAP: *Generally Accepted Accounting Procedures* are the common set of accounting principles, standards and procedures established by the Financial Accounting Standards Board that companies use to compile their Financial Statements.

Going Concern Value: The value of a business enterprise that is expected to continue to operate into the future. The intangible elements of Going Concern Value result from factors such as having a trained work force, an operational plant, and the necessary licenses, systems, and procedures in place.

Goodwill: That intangible asset arising as a result of name, reputation, customer loyalty, location, products, and similar factors not separately identified.

Goodwill Value: The value attributable to goodwill. An intangible asset which provides a competitive advantage, such as a strong brand and reputation.

Growth Capital: An investment made in an operating company by an outside investor to support existing or anticipated expansion of the business. May or may not include a change of equity control, but it frequently involves the exchange of equity ownership.

Indemnification: A contractual term whereby one party agrees to compensate the other party for any loss that the other party may suffer related to the contract or transaction. In stock and asset purchase agreements, it is typical for one party to indemnify the other party for a breach of Representations and Warranties made by such party.

Intangible Assets: Nonphysical assets (such as franchises, trademarks, patents, copyrights, goodwill, equities, mineral rights, securities and contracts as distinguished from physical assets) that grant rights, privileges, and have economic benefits for the owner.

Intermediary: A merger & acquisition advisor who assists buyers and sellers of privately held small businesses throughout the business transfer transaction process.

Investment Banker: An individual who works in a financial institution that is in the business primarily of raising capital for companies, governments and other entities, or who works in a large bank's division that is involved with these activities. Investment bankers may also provide other services to their clients such as mergers and acquisition advice, or advice on specific transactions, such as a spin-off or reorganization.

Key Person Discount: An amount or percentage deducted from the value of an ownership interest to reflect the reduction in value resulting from the actual or potential loss of a key person in a business enterprise.

Letter of Intent (LOI): A formal, written document indicating the terms a buyer is offering a seller in a proposed acquisition or investment. Although not a contract, it is a document stating serious intent to carry out the proposed acquisition.

Liquidity: The ability to quickly convert property to cash or pay a liability.

Liquidation Value: The net amount that can be realized if the business is terminated and the assets are sold piecemeal. Liquidation can be either "orderly" or "forced."

M&A: An abbreviation for "mergers & acquisitions," which generally refers to the buying and selling of companies, or the combination of two companies in which only one of the companies survives. Acquisitions can be asset purchases, where the buyer purchases the seller's assets, without assuming any liabilities, or stock purchases, where the buyer purchases the business's stock and takes over the seller's business.

Majority Control: The degree of control provided by a majority position.

Majority Interest: An ownership interest greater than fifty percent (50%) of the voting interest in a business enterprise.

Management Buy-out: A process whereby management of a company acquires all or some of the ownership of the company they manage either independently or in partnership with a private equity fund/group (PEG).

Merger: The combination of two or more companies, either through (1) a pooling of interests in which the accounts are combined, (2) a purchase where the amount paid over and above the acquired company's book value is carried on the books of the purchaser as goodwill, or (3) a consolidation in which a new company is formed to acquire the net assets of the combining companies.

Minority Discount: A discount for lack of control applicable to a minority interest.

Minority Interest: An ownership interest less than fifty percent (50%) of the voting interest in a business enterprise.

Net Book Value: With respect to a business enterprise, the difference between total assets (net of accumulated depreciation, depletion, and amortization) and total liabilities of a business enterprise as they appear on the balance sheet (synonymous with *shareholder's equity*); with respect to an intangible asset, the capitalized cost of an intangible asset less accumulated amortization as it appears on the accounting books of the business enterprise.

Net Tangible Asset Value: The value of the business enterprise's tangible assets (excluding excess assets and non-operating assets) minus the value of its liabilities.

Non-Disclosure Agreement: An agreement to protect confidential information being disclosed to a prospective investor or acquirer. Also called an "NDA" or "Confidentiality Agreement" or "CA."

Non-operating Assets: Assets not necessary to ongoing operations of the business enterprise.

Orderly Liquidation Value: Liquidation value at which the asset or assets are sold over a reasonable period of time to maximize proceeds received.

Premise of Value: An assumption regarding the most likely set of transactional circumstances that may be applicable to the subject valuation; e.g. going concern, liquidation.

Private Equity: An investment in non-public securities of, typically, private companies. Also, an investment asset class typically reserved for large institutional investors such as pension funds and endowments as well as high net worth individuals. Includes investments in privately-held companies ranging from start-up companies to well-established and profitable companies to bankrupt or near bankrupt companies. Examples of private equity include venture capital, leveraged buyout, growth capital and distressed investments.

Private Equity Fund: An investment vehicle, typically a Limited Partnership, formed to make investments in private companies via a pool of available equity capital.

PEG: A private equity group.

Portfolio Discount: An amount or percentage that may be deducted from the value of a business enterprise to reflect the fact that it owns dissimilar operations or assets that may not fit well together.

Portfolio Company: A company acquired and owned by a private equity fund.

Promissory Note: A promissory note is a form of debt that a maker/debtor issues to raise money or pay as consideration in an acquisition.

Rate of Return: An amount of income (loss) and/or change in value realized or anticipated on an investment, expressed as a percentage of that investment.

Recapitalization: A financing transaction that allow owners to harvest some of the value they have created in their companies while retaining a large ownership stake in the business going forward.

Representations & Warranties: Statements of fact and assurances by one party to the other party that certain facts or conditions are true or will be true at closing, and often after the closing.

Risk Premium: A rate of return in addition to a risk-free rate to compensate the investor for accepting risk.

Search Fund: An individual or group of individuals seeking to identify an acquisition candidate that the individual or group can acquire and subsequently manage.

Sustaining Capital Reinvestment: The periodic capital outlay required to maintain operations at existing levels, net of the tax shield available from such outlays.

Systematic Risk: The risk that is common to all risky securities and cannot be eliminated through diversification.

Term Sheet: A document setting forth the terms of a proposed acquisition, merger or securities offering. A term sheet may take the form of a "Letter of Intent."

Valuation: The act or process of determining the value of a business, business ownership interest, security, or intangible asset.

Valuation Approach: A general way of determining a value indication of a business, business ownership interest, security, or intangible asset using one or more valuation methods.

Valuation Date: The specific point in time as of which the valuator's opinion of value applies, also referred to as "Effective Date" or "Appraisal Date."

Weighted Average Cost of Capital (WACC): The cost of capital (discount rate) determined by the weighted average at market value of the cost of all financing sources in the business enterprise's capital structure.

Sources:

http://www.DealFirm.com

http://www.MAsource.org/page/Glossary

http://www.MergerMarket.com

https://CorporateFinanceInstitute.com

Notes

Notes

Notes

Notes

Notes

Notes

Notes

www.ingramcontent.com/pod-product-compliance
Lightning Source LLC
Chambersburg PA
CBHW021411210526
45463CB00001B/319